The Story of the

A Book About Mountains for General Readers.

H. N. Hutchinson

Alpha Editions

This edition published in 2024

ISBN : 9789362994059

Design and Setting By
Alpha Editions
www.alphaedis.com
Email - info@alphaedis.com

As per information held with us this book is in Public Domain.
This book is a reproduction of an important historical work. Alpha Editions uses the best technology to reproduce historical work in the same manner it was first published to preserve its original nature. Any marks or number seen are left intentionally to preserve its true form.

Contents

PREFACE. ....- 1 -

PART I. THE MOUNTAINS AS THEY ARE. ....- 3 -

CHAPTER I. MOUNTAINS AND MEN. ....- 5 -

CHAPTER II. THE USES OF MOUNTAINS. ....- 18 -

CHAPTER III. SUNSHINE AND STORM ON THE MOUNTAINS. ....- 35 -

CHAPTER IV. MOUNTAIN PLANTS AND ANIMALS. ....- 50 -

PART II. HOW THE MOUNTAINS WERE MADE. ....- 65 -

CHAPTER V. HOW THE MATERIALS WERE BROUGHT TOGETHER. ....- 67 -

CHAPTER VI. HOW THE MOUNTAINS WERE UPHEAVED. ....- 82 -

CHAPTER VII. HOW THE MOUNTAINS WERE CARVED OUT. ....- 96 -

CHAPTER VIII. VOLCANIC MOUNTAINS. ....- 112 -

CHAPTER IX. MOUNTAIN ARCHITECTURE. ....- 129 -

CHAPTER X. THE AGES OF MOUNTAINS, AND OTHER QUESTIONS. ....- 145 -

FOOTNOTES: ....- 160 -

PREFACE.

Now that travelling is no longer a luxury for the rich, and thousands of people go every summer to spend their holidays among the mountains of Europe, and ladies climb Mont Blanc or ramble among the Carpathians, there must be many who would like to know something of the secret of the hills, their origin, their architecture, and the forces that made them what they are.

For such this book is chiefly written. Those will best understand it who take it with them on their travels, and endeavour by its use to interpret what they see among the mountains; and they will find that a little observation goes a long way to help them to read mountain history.

It is hoped, however, that all, both young and old, who take an intelligent interest in the world around, though they may never have seen a mountain, may find these pages worth reading.

If readers do not find here answers to all their questions, they may be reminded that it is not possible within the present limits to give more than a brief sketch of the subject, leaving the gaps to be filled in by a study of the larger and more important works on geology. The author, assuming that the reader knows nothing of this fascinating science, has endeavoured to interpret into ordinary language the story of the hills as it is written in the rocks of which they are made.

It can scarcely be denied that a little knowledge of natural objects greatly adds to our appreciation of them, besides affording a deep source of pleasure, in revealing the harmony, law, and order by which all things in this wonderful world are governed. Mountains, when once we begin to observe them, seem to become more than ever our companions,—to take us into their counsels, and to teach us many a lesson about the great part they play in the order of things. And surely our admiration of their beauty is not lessened, but rather increased, when we learn how much we and all living things owe to the life-giving streams that flow continually from them. The writer has, somewhat reluctantly, omitted certain parts of the subject which, though very interesting to the geologist, can hardly be made attractive to general readers.

Thus, the cause of earth movements, by which mountains are pushed up far above the plains that lie at their feet, is at present a matter of speculation; and it is difficult to express in ordinary language the ideas that have been put forward on this subject. Again, the curious internal changes, which we find to have taken place in the rocks of which mountains are composed, are very interesting to those who know something of the minerals of which rocks are made up, and their chemical composition; but it was found impossible to render these matters sufficiently simple.

So again with regard to the geological structure of mountain-chains. This had to be very briefly treated, in order to avoid introducing details which would be too complicated for a book of this kind.

The author desires to acknowledge his obligations to the writings of Sir A. Geikie; Professor Bonney, Professor Green, and Professor Shaler, of Harvard University; the volumes of the "Alpine Journal;" "The Earth," by Reclus; the "Encyclopædia Britannica." Canon Isaac Taylor's "Words and Places," have also been made use of; and if in every case the reference is not given, the writer hopes the omission will be pardoned. A few passages from Mr. Ruskin's "Modern Painters" have been quoted, in the hope that others may be led to read that wonderful book, and to learn more about mountains and clouds, and many other things, at the feet of one of the greatest teachers of the century.

Some of our engravings are taken from the justly celebrated photographs of the High Alps,[1] by the late Mr. W. Donkin, whose premature death among the Caucasus Mountains was xi deeply deplored by all. Those reproduced were kindly lent by his brother, Mr. A. E. Donkin, of Rugby. To Messrs. Valentine & Son of Dundee, Mr. Wilson of Aberdeen, and to Messrs. Frith we are indebted for permission to reproduce some of their admirable photographs; also to Messrs. James How & Sons of Farringdon Street, for three excellent photographs of rock-sections taken with the microscope.

PART I.
THE MOUNTAINS AS THEY ARE.

CHAPTER I.
MOUNTAINS AND MEN.

"Happy, I said, whose home is here; Fair fortunes to the Mountaineer."

In old times people looked with awe upon the mountains, and regarded them with feelings akin to horror or dread. A very slight acquaintance with the classical writers of antiquity will suffice to convince any one that Greeks and Romans did so regard them. They were not so familiar with mountains as we are; for there were no roads through them, as now through the Alps, or the Highlands of Scotland,—to say nothing of the all-pervading railway. It would, however, be a great mistake to suppose that the ancients did not observe and enjoy the beauties of Nature. The fair and fertile plain, the vine-clad slopes of the lower hill-ranges, and the "many-twinkling smile of ocean" were seen and loved by all who had a mind to appreciate the beautiful. The poems of Homer and Virgil would alone be sufficient to prove this. But the higher ranges, untrodden by the foot of man, were gazed at, not with admiration, but with religious awe; for men looked upon mountains as the abode of the gods. They dwelt in the rich plain, which they cultivated, and beside the sweet waters of some river; for food and drink are the first necessities of life. But they left the high hills alone, and in fancy peopled them with the "Immortals" who ruled their destiny,—controlling also the winds and the lightning, the rain and the clouds, which seem to have their home among the mountains. A childlike fear of the unknown, coupled with religious awe, made them avoid the lofty and barren hills, from which little was to be got but wild honey and a scanty supply of game. There were also dangers to be encountered from the fury of the storm and the avalanche; but the safer ground of the plains below would reward their toil with an ample supply of corn and other necessaries of life.

In classical times, and also in the Middle Ages, the mountains, as well as glens and rivers, were supposed to be peopled with fairies, nymphs, elves, and all sorts of strange beings; and even now travellers among the mountains of Switzerland, Norway, Wales, or Scotland find that it is not long since the simple folk of these regions believed in the existence of such beings, and attributed to their agency many things which they could not otherwise explain.

Of all the nations of antiquity the Jews seem to have shown the greatest appreciation of mountain scenery; and in no ancient writings do we find so many or so eloquent allusions to the hills as in the Old Testament. But here again one cannot fail to trace the same feelings of religious awe. The Law was given to their forefathers in the desert amidst the thunders of Sinai. To them the earth was literally Jehovah's footstool, and the clouds were His tabernacle. "If He do but touch the hills, they shall smoke."

But this awe was not unmixed with other and more comforting thoughts. They felt that those cloud-capped towers were symbols of strength and the abode of Him who would help them in their need. For so we find the psalmists regarding them; and with our very different conceptions of the earth's natural features, we can but dimly perceive and realise the full force and meaning of the words, "I will lift up mine eyes unto the hills, from whence cometh my help."

To take another example from antiquity, we find that the Himalayas and the source of the Ganges have from very early times been considered as holy by the people of India. Thousands of pilgrims from all parts of that vast country still continue to seek salvation in the holy waters of the Ganges, and at its sacred sources in the snowy Himalayas. And to those who know India the wondrous snowclad peaks of the Himalayas still seem to be surrounded with somewhat of the same halo of glory as of old.

Mountains are intimately associated with the history of nations, and have contributed much to the moulding of the human mind and the character of those who dwell among them; they have alike inspired the mind of the artist, the poet, the reformer, and the visionary seeking repose for his soul, that, dwelling far from the strife and turmoil of the world, he may contemplate alone the glory of the Eternal Being. They have been the refuge of the afflicted and the persecuted; they have braced the minds and bodies of heroes who have dwelt for a time among them before descending once more to the plain that they might play some noble part in the progress of the world.

Moses, while leading the flock of his father-in-law to the back of the wilderness, came to Mount Horeb and received the divine summons to return to Egypt and lead Israel out of bondage. David, with his six hundred followers, fleeing from the face of Saul, found a refuge in the hill country; and the life of peril and adventure which he led during these years of persecution was a part of his training for the great future task of ruling Israel, which he performed so well. Elijah summoned the false prophets of Baal and Asherah to Mount Carmel and slew them at the brook Kishon; and a little later we find him at Mount Horeb listening, not to the wind or to the earthquake or to the fire, but to the "still small voice" telling him to return and anoint Jehu to be king.

Or, to take another example from a later age, we find that Mahomet's favourite resort was a cave at the foot of Mount Hira, north of Mecca; here in dark and wild surroundings his mind was wrought up to rhapsodic enthusiasm.

And many, like these leaders of men, have received in mountain retreats a firmness and tenacity of purpose giving them the right to be leaders, and the power to redress human wrongs; or, it may be, a temper of mind and spirit enabling them to soar into regions of thought and contemplation untrodden by the careless and more luxurious multitudes who dwell on the plains below. Perhaps Mr. Lewis Morris was unconsciously offering his testimony to the influence of mountains when he wrote those words which he puts into the mouth of poor Marsyas,—

"More it is than ease,

Palace and pomp, honours and luxuries,

To have seen white presences upon the hills,

To have heard the voices of the eternal gods."[2]

The thunder and lightning, storm and cloud, as well as the soft beauty of colour, and the harmony of mountain outline, have been a part, and a very important part, of their training. The exhilarating air, the struggle with the elements in their fierceness, the rugged strength of granite, seem to have possessed the very souls of such men, and made them like "the strong ones,"—the immortal beings to whom in all previous ages the races of mankind have assigned their abode in the hills, as the Greek gods were supposed to dwell on Mount Olympus. On these heights such men seem to have gained something of the strength of Him who dwells in the heavens far above their highest peaks,—"the strength of the hills," which, as the Hebrew poet says, "is His also."

We have spoken of the attitude of the human mind towards mountains in the past; let us now consider the light in which they are regarded at the present time by all thoughtful and cultivated people. And it does not require a moment's consideration to perceive that a very great change has taken place. Instead of regarding them with horror or aversion, we look upon them with wonder and delight; we watch them hour by hour whenever for a brief season of holiday we take up our abode near or among them. We come back to them year by year to breathe once more the pure air which so frequently restores the invalid to health and brings back the colour to faded cheeks. We love to watch the ever-varying lights and shades upon them, as the day goes by. But it is towards evening that the most enchanting scenes are to be witnessed, when the sinking sun sheds its golden rays upon their slopes, or tinges their summits with floods of crimson light; and then presently, after the sun has gone down, pale mists begin to rise, and the hills seem more majestic than ever. Later on, as the full moon appears from behind a bank of cloud, those wonderful moonlight effects may be seen which must be familiar to all who know the mountains as they are in summer or autumn,—scenes such as the writer has frequently witnessed in the Highlands of Scotland, but which only the poet can adequately describe.

There are few sights in Nature which more powerfully impress the mind than a sunset among the mountains. General Sir Richard Strachey concludes his description of the Himalayas with the following striking passage:

"Here may the eye, as it sweeps along the horizon, embrace a line of snowclad mountains such as exist in no other part of the world, stretching over one third of the entire circle, at a distance of forty or fifty miles, their peaks towering over a sea of intervening ranges piled one behind another, whose extent on either hand is lost in the remote distance, and of which the nearest rises from a gulf far down beneath the spectator's feet, where may be seen the silver line that marks a river's course, or crimson fields of amaranth and the dwellings of man. Sole representative of animal life, some great eagle floats high overhead in the pure dark-blue sky, or, unused to man, fearlessly sweeps down within a few yards to gaze at the stranger who intrudes among these solitudes of Nature. As the sun sinks, the cold grey shadow of the summit where we stand is thrown forward, slowly stealing over the distant hills, and veiling their glowing purples as it goes, carries the night up to the feet of the great snowy peaks, which still rise radiant in the rosy light above the now darkening world. From east to west in succession the splendour fades away from one point after another, and the vast shadow of the earth is rapidly drawn across the whole vault of heaven. One more departing day is added to the countless series which has silently witnessed the deathlike change that passes over the eternal snows, as they are left raising their cold pale fronts against the now leaden sky; till slowly with the deepening night the world of mountains rises again, as it were, to a new life, under the changed light of the thousand stars which stud the firmament and shine with a brilliancy unknown except in the clear rarefied air of these sublime heights."

Year by year a larger number of busy workers from our great towns, availing themselves of the increased facilities for travel, come to the mountains to spend their summer holidays,—some to the Swiss Alps, others to Wales, Cumberland, Norway, or the Highlands of Scotland. There are few untrodden valleys in these regions, few of the more important mountains which have not been climbed.

Our knowledge of mountains, thanks to the labours of a zealous army of workers, is now considerable. The professors of physical science have been busy making important observations on the condition of the atmosphere in the higher regions; geographers have noted their heights and mapped their leading contours. Geologists have done a vast amount of work in ascertaining the composition and arrangement of the rocks of which mountain chains are composed, in observing their peculiar structures, in recording the changes which are continually effecting their waste and decay, and thus interpreting the story of the hills as it is written in the very rocks of which they are built up.

Naturalists have collected and noted the peculiar plants and animals which have their home among the hills, and so the forms of life, both animal and vegetable, which inhabit the mountains of Europe, and some other countries, are now fairly well known.

The historian, the antiquary, and the student of languages have made interesting discoveries with regard to the mountain races of mankind. And only to mention this country, such writers as Scott, Wordsworth, and Ruskin have given us in verse and prose descriptions of mountain scenery which will take a permanent place in literature; while Turner, our great landscape-painter, has expressed the glories of mountain scenery in pictures which speak more eloquently than many words. Thus we see that whatever line of inquiry be chosen, our subject is full of varied interest.

With regard to the characteristics of mountain races, it is not easy to say to what extent people in different parts of the world who live among mountains share the same virtues or the same failings; but the most obvious traits in the character of the mountaineer seem to be the result of his natural surroundings. Thus we find mountaineers generally endowed with hardihood, strength, and bravery. To spend one's days on the hillsides for a large part of the year, as shepherds and others do in Scotland or Wales, and to walk some miles every day in pure bracing air, must be healthy and tend to develop the muscles of the body; and so we find the highlanders of all countries are usually muscular, strong, and capable of endurance. And there can be little doubt that mountain races are kept up to a high standard of strength and endurance by a rigorous and constant weeding out of the weakly ones, especially among children. And if only the stronger live to grow up and become parents, the chances are that their children will be strong too. Thus Nature exercises a kind of "selection;" and we have consequently "the survival of the fittest." This "selection," together with the healthy lives they lead, is probably sufficient to account for their strength and hardiness.

As might be expected, mountaineers are celebrated for their fighting qualities. The fierce Afghans who have often faced a British army, and sometimes victoriously; the brave Swiss peasantry, who have more than once fought nobly for freedom; the Highlanders, who have contributed so largely to the success of British arms in nearly all parts of the world, and whose forefathers defied even the all-conquering Roman in their mountain strongholds,—these and many others all show the same valour and power of endurance. Etymologists, whose learned researches into the meaning of words have thrown so much light on the ages before history was written, tell us that the Picts were so called from their fighting qualities, and that the word "Pict" is derived from the Gaelic "peicta," a fighting man. And Julius Cæsar says the chief god of the Britons was the god of war.

In some countries—as, for instance, Greece, Italy, and Spain—the mountains are infested with banditti and robbers, who often become a terror to the neighbourhood. In more peaceful and orderly countries, however, we find among mountaineers many noble qualities,—such as patience, honesty, simplicity of life, thrift, a dignified self-reliance, together with true courtesy and hospitality. This is high praise; but who that knows mountain peasants would say it is undeserved? How many a tired traveller among the hills of Scotland or Wales has had reason to be grateful for welcome, food, and rest in some little cottage in a far-away glen! How many friendships have thus been formed! How many a pleasant talk has beguiled the time during a storm or shower! The old feuds are forgotten now that the Saxon stranger and invader is at peace with the Celtic people whom his forefathers drove into the hills. The castles, once centres of oppression or scenes of violence, lie in peaceful and picturesque ruins, and add not a little to the interest of one's travels in the North. What true courtesy and consideration one meets with at the hands of these honest folk, among whom the old kindly usages have not died out! Often too poor to be afflicted with the greed and thirst for wealth, which frequently marks the man of the plain as compared with the man of the hills,—the Lowlander as compared with the Highlander,—they exhibit many of those simple virtues which one hardly expects to meet with among busy townspeople, all bent on making money, or as the phrase is, "getting on in life."

BEN LOMOND. F**ROM A** P**HOTOGRAPH BY** J. V**ALENTINE**

"The mountain cheer, the frosty skies,

Breed purer wits, inventive eyes;

And then the moral of the place

Hints summits of heroic grace.

Men in these crags a fastness find

To fight corruption of the mind;

The insanity of towns to stem

With simpleness for stratagem."

Mr. Skene, the Scotch historian, records a touching case of the devotion of Highlanders to their chief. He says,—

"There is perhaps no instance in which the attachment of the clan to their chief was so strongly manifested as in the case of the Macphersons of Cluny after the disaster of 'the Forty-five.' The chief having been deeply engaged in that insurrection, his life became of course forfeited to the laws; but neither the hope of reward nor the fear of danger could induce any one of his people to betray him. For nine years he lived concealed in a cave a short distance from his own house; it was situated in the front of a woody precipice of which the trees and shelving rocks concealed the entrance. The cave had been dug by his own people, who worked at night and conveyed the stones and rubbish into a neighbouring lake, in order that no vestige of their labour might appear and lead to the discovery of the retreat. In this asylum he continued to live secure, receiving by night the occasional visits of his friends, and sometimes by day, when the soldiers had begun to slacken the vigour of their pursuit. Upwards of one thousand persons were privy to his concealment, and a reward of £1,000 was offered to any one who should give information against him.... But although the soldiers were animated by the hope of reward, and their officers by promise of promotion for the apprehension of this proscribed individual, yet so true were his people, so inflexibly strict in their promise of secrecy, and so dextrous in conveying to him the necessaries he required in his long confinement, not a trace of him could be discovered, nor an individual base enough to give a hint to his detriment."

The mountaineer is a true gentleman. However poor, however ignorant or superstitious, one perceives in him a refinement of manner which cannot fail to command admiration. His readiness to share his best with the stranger and to render any service in his power are pleasing traits in his character. But there is one sad feature about mountaineers of the present day which one frequently notices in districts where many tourists come,— especially English or American. They are, we regret to say, losing their independence, their simple, old-fashioned ways, and becoming servile and greedy,—at least in the towns and villages. Such changes seem, alas! inevitable when rich townspeople, bent on pleasure or sport, invade the recesses of the hills where poverty usually reigns. On the one hand, we have people, often with long purses, eager for enjoyment, waiting to be fed, housed, or otherwise entertained; on the other hand, poor people, anxious to "make hay while the sun shines" and to extract as much money as possible from "the visitors," who often allow themselves to be unmercifully fleeced. Then there are in the Highlands the sportsmen, who require a large following of "gillies" to attend them in their wanderings, pay them highly for their services, and dismiss them at the end of the season; and so the men are in many cases left without employment all the winter and spring. Is it, then, surprising that they give way to a natural tendency to idleness, and fall into other bad habits? Any visitor who spends a winter, or part of one, in the Highlands will be better able to realise the extent of this evil, which is by no means small; and one cannot help regretting that the sportsmen's pleasure and the tourist's holiday should involve results of such grave consequence. We are inclined to think that in these days sport is overdone, and wish it could be followed without taking the hillman away from the work he would otherwise find, and which would render him a more useful member of society. With the agitation going on in some parts against deer-forests we do not feel much sympathy, because they are based on the erroneous idea that "crofters" could make a living out of the land thus enclosed; whereas those who know the land and its value for agricultural purposes tell us that with the exception of a few small patches here and there, hardly worth mentioning, it could not possibly be made to produce enough to maintain crofters and their families. Nevertheless, another way of looking at the matter is this: that the man who merely ministers to the pleasure of others richer than himself loses some of the self-respect and independence which he would acquire by working in his own way for a living.

The same changes for the worse are still more manifest in Switzerland; and even in some parts of Norway the people are being similarly spoiled. Mr. Ruskin, speaking of the former country, says:

"I believe that every franc now spent by travellers among the Alps tends more or less to the undermining of whatever special greatness there is in the Swiss character; and the persons I met in Switzerland whose position and modes of life render them best able to give me true information respecting the present state of their country, among many causes of national deterioration, spoke with chief fear of the influx of English wealth, gradually connecting all industry with the wants of strangers, and inviting all idleness to depend upon their casual help, thus resolving the ancient consistency and pastoral simplicity of the mountain life into the two irregular trades of the innkeeper and mendicant."[3]

Mountain people have still their superstitions; since the introduction of railways many of the old legends and popular myths have died out, but even what is left is interesting to the student of folk-lore,—indeed, we might say, to every one.

Sir A. Geikie, speaking of Scotch mountain scenery says,—

"To the influence of scenery of this kind on the mind of a people at once observant and imaginative, such legends as that of the Titans should in all likelihood be ascribed. It would be interesting to trace back these legends to their cradle, and to mark how much they owe to the character of the scenery amongst which they took their rise. Perhaps it would be found that the rugged outlines of the Bœotian hills had no small share in the framing of Hesiod's graphic story of that primeval warfare wherein the combatants fought with huge rocks, which, darkening the air as they flew, at last buried the discomfited Titans deep beneath the surface of the land. Nor would it be difficult to trace a close connection between the present scenery of our own country and some of the time-honoured traditionary stories of giants and hero kings, warlocks and witches, or between the doings of the Scandinavian Hrimthursar, or Frost Giants, and the more characteristic features of the landscapes and climate of the North."[4]

The following passage from Ruskin brings out more strongly the effects of mountains on men,—a subject to which he has given much attention:—

"We shall find, on the one hand, the mountains of Greece and Italy, forming all the loveliest dreams, first of Pagan, then of Christian mythology, on the other, those of Scandinavia, to be the first sources of whatever mental (as well as military) power was brought by the Normans into Southern Europe. Normandy itself is, to all intents and purposes, a hill country.... We have thus one branch of the Northern religious imagination rising among the Scandinavian fiords, tempered in France by various encounters with elements of Arabian, Italian, Provençal, or other Southern poetry, and then reacting upon Southern England; while other forms of the same rude religious imagination, resting like clouds upon the mountains of Scotland and Wales, met and mingled with the Norman Christianity, retaining even to the latest times some dark colour of superstition, but giving all its poetical and military pathos to Scottish poetry, and a peculiar sternness and wildness of tone to the Reformed faith, in its manifestations among the Scottish hills."[5]

The Alps, like most other mountainous countries, have their fair share of legends, some of which are very grotesque. We have selected the following, as related by Professor Bonney.[6] The wild huntsman's yell is still heard in many places by the shuddering peasants as his phantom train sweeps by the châlet. There is also the wild goat-herd, a wicked lad, who crucified an old he-goat and drove his flock to worship it; lightning consumed him; and now he wanders forever over the Alps, miserably wailing.

When the glacier of Gétroz burst, the Archfiend himself was seen swimming down the Rhone, with a drawn sword in one hand and a golden ball in the other; when opposite to Martigny he halted, and at his bidding the waters rose and swept away part of the town. A vast multitude of imps was seen about the same time on a mountain in the Val de Bagnes by two mendicant friars from Sion, who, hearing of this unlawful assembly, had gone out as detectives to learn what mischief was hatching.

Many places also have their spectral animals, the Valois, according to Tschudi, being the headquarters of these legends. There are also pygmies to be seen in the lonely mountains, like the Norwegian trolls, and brownies who make or mar the house, according as the goodwife is neat or a slattern.

Many Alpine stories have reference to the sudden destruction of pastures by the fall of rocks or ice. Here is one from the Clariden Alps:—

Once upon a time these were fertile pastures, on which dwelt a "senn." He grew rich, so that none could match him in wealth; but at the same time he grew proud and haughty, and spurned both the laws of Nature and the commandments of God. He was so foolishly fond of his mistress that he paved the way from the châlet to the byre with cheeses, lest she should soil her feet, and cared so little for his mother that when she lay at his door fainting with hunger, he offered her only milk to drink in which he had thrown the foulest refuse. Righteously indignant, she turned away, calling upon Heaven to punish such an insult. Before she reached her home, the rocks and ice had descended, crushing beneath them her wicked son, his mistress, and possessions.

In the neighbourhood of Monte Rosa there is a tradition that a valley exists in the heart of that mountain the entrance to which has been sealed up by impassable glaciers, though the floor of the "cirque" within is still a rich pasturage. In a certain valley they point out a spring which bursts from the ground, as the outlet of the torrent by which it is watered. Once, said they, a chasseur found the bed of this stream dry, and creeping up its subterranean channel, arrived on the floor of the valley. It was a huntsman's paradise; chamois were there in plenty, bears also, and even bouquetins, wandering over the richest pastures. He retraced his steps to announce the good news; but when he returned again, the waters had resumed their course, and the place has ever since remained inaccessible.

Mountains play a very important part in human history. In the first place, they are natural barriers separating the nations of the world from one another, and tending to keep them confined within certain definite bounds; we say, tending to keep them thus confined, because, as every one knows, these barriers have again and again been surmounted by conquering armies. The rugged Alps could not ward off Hannibal, who made his way through them to march upon the capital of the Roman empire. In like manner Napoleon defied this great natural rampart, made a road through it, and came to Italy. No mountains would seem to be quite impassable; but although liable in the course of ages to be occasionally overrun, they afford good protection and produce a feeling of security.

The Himalayas separate our great Indian empire from that of China; and we do not at present apprehend an invasion from that quarter. The Suliman Mountains divide us from the Afghans, and the great Russian and Persian empires farther west. Still, we know that in the eleventh century a great Mahometan invasion of India took place; our own armies have more than once penetrated to Kabul. Perhaps the common garden wall separating adjacent suburban residences furnishes a suitable illustration of the great natural walls which divide, not households or families, but much larger families than these,—the nations of the world.

Just as unruly boys sometimes climb over the neighbour's wall and play games in a garden which is not their own; or as burglars may surmount these obstacles to their progress, and finding a way into the house by a back door or kitchen window, commence their ravages,—so a neighbouring (but not neighbourly) nation, bent on conquest, may invade some natural garden of the world, such as India, by forcing their way through physical barriers which for ordinary purposes serve to protect those within.

The Thian Shan Mountains divide Russia from China's sphere of influence. The Caucasus Mountains separate Russia from Asia Minor. Austro-Hungary is bounded by the Carpathians, Spain by the Pyrenees. The Alps of Switzerland separate four nations not very friendly to each other; and lastly, in our own country the Cheviot Hills, together with the Tweed, form the boundary between Scotland and England.

Where there are no mountains or hills, rivers sometimes serve as boundaries, but of course they do not answer the purpose so well. Sometimes a nation actually builds a wall for a boundary. Of this the great wall of China and the Roman wall between the Cheviots and the Solway Firth are familiar examples.

In the second place, mountains have always been a refuge and shelter for conquered races; and the primitive tribes who once lived in the plains have been forced by adverse circumstances to take to the hills. This has taken place over and over again.

We know that the Celtic people now living in Brittany, Devonshire, Cornwall, Wales, Scotland, and Ireland, though now considerably mixed, are the descendants of the old Celtic inhabitants of France and Britain. But there is a great deal of unwritten history for which we may look in vain to the ordinary sources of information, such as books, and which is only to be read in quite different records,—in antiquities buried up in peat-beds, in bogs, in ruins and ancient forts, or camps; and last but not least, in the names of places, rivers, or mountains. The hills, the valleys, the rivers, are the only writing-tablets on which unlettered nations have been able to inscribe their annals. For this kind of history we must go to the antiquary, and, above all, to the philologist, who tells us the meaning of the names of places, and who the people were who gave the names that we see on our maps. The great advances which have of late years been made in our knowledge of the primeval races of men, or at least of nations but little known in the annals of history, are largely due to the interpretation of the obscure records preserved in local names. The Celtic, the Iberian, the Teutonic, the Scandinavian, and Sclavonic races have thus for the most part made known to us their migrations, conquests, and defeats. And so by studying the names of places, rivers, and hills, as well as by careful collection of works of art, implements, coins, such as may be seen in many a museum, it has been possible to read a great deal of early history which would otherwise have been lost.

Those who have studied these matters say they can trace wave after wave of population which has thus left its mark,—Gaelic, Cymric (or Welsh), Saxon, Anglian, Norwegian, Danish, Norman, and Flemish. Thus it can be proved from the names on the map that almost the whole of England was once Celtic, whereas now the Celts are almost entirely confined to the hills. The Peak of Derbyshire and the mountains of Cumberland retain a greater number of Celtic names than the districts surrounding them; and the hills of Devonshire long served as a barrier to protect the Celts of Cornwall from Anglo-Saxon conquerors.

But even mountain races are often a good deal mixed, and in the Pyrenees we find the descendants of the Iberians, who, a very long time ago, were driven from the lowlands of France and Spain. These Iberians are a very interesting race, of short stature, with long heads, and dark hair and eyes. This old type is to be met with in Wales and the Highlands even in the present day. And so we learn—if these conclusions are sound—that even the Celts in their early days were invaders, and drove before them an older population. This race, it seems, lived in Europe a very long time ago, before the discovery of metals, when people made axes, hammers, and spear-heads out of flints or other stones; and so they are said to belong to "the Stone Age." Their remains are found in many of the caves which of late years have been explored. Possibly the ancient people of Switzerland who lived in wooden houses, erected on piles near the shores of lakes (probably for safety), were also of the same stock. It is curious to find how people living in separate valleys among the mountains of Switzerland have, in the course of time, become so much unlike their neighbours that they can hardly understand each other's speech, so effectually have the mountains kept them apart. In some districts almost every valley has its separate dialect. Switzerland is only twice the size of Wales, yet the local names are derived from half a dozen different languages, three or four of which are still spoken by the people. In the Alps, too, the same mixture of Celtic with an older Iberian stock has been detected. A curious reversal of the usual order of things is noticed by the late Dean Stanley in his "Sinai and Palestine." He points out that the Jews took possession of many of the hills of Palestine soon after the invasion under Joshua, but could not drive out the peoples of the plains, because they were better armed, and had chariots of iron in great number. The conquerors in this case kept to the hills; while the Canaanites, Philistines, and other inhabitants of the country retained for a long time their hold of the lower ground.

CHAPTER II.
THE USES OF MOUNTAINS.

The valleys only feed; the mountains feed and guard and strengthen us.—RUSKIN.

It is not an exaggeration to say that there are no physical features of the surface of the earth which render such a variety of services as mountains. The operations which they perform involve such far-reaching consequences that it is difficult to say where their effects cease. Indeed, it might almost be maintained that they are the mainspring of the world,—as far as its surface is concerned,—for it would fare ill with mankind if they were removed or in some way destroyed. Things would then very soon come to a standstill. The soil would become exhausted; streams would cease to flow; and the world would become a kind of stagnant pool.

The three main services of the hills are these:—

1.   I. Mountains help to condense water-vapour from the atmosphere, thus bringing back to the earth moisture which it loses continually by evaporation.

2.   Mountains are elevated reservoirs of water in II. one form or another, and thus not only feed the streams and rivers, but give them force and direction as well.

3.   III. Mountains suffer themselves to be slowly worn away in order that the face of the earth may be renewed; in other words, they die that we, and all created things, may live.

I. Mountains help to condense water-vapour from the atmosphere, thus bringing back to the earth the moisture which it loses continually by evaporation. Every one knows that there is abundance of water-vapour in the atmosphere, but the question arises, How does it get there? The answer to this lies in the simple fact that every surface of water exposed to the air undergoes loss by evaporation. If you wish to satisfy yourself on this point, place a saucer of water in your room, and in a few days it will all be gone. We hang clothes out to dry, and so avail ourselves of this curious power that air has of taking up water in the form of vapour. Steam, or water-vapour, is really invisible, though we frequently talk of seeing the steam issuing from a locomotive; but what we really see is a cloud of condensed steam, and such clouds,[7] like those that we see floating in the air, are really masses of little tiny particles of water which can reflect or throw back the light which falls upon them, and thus they become visible. Again, a kettle of water, if left too long on the fire will entirely boil away. It is all turned into steam, and the steam is somehow hidden away in the air, though a little of it will be condensed into slight clouds by the colder air outside the kettle.

But how can water stow itself away in the air without being seen or felt?

An illustration may help to explain this. Suppose you scatter a spoonful of small shot over a carpet or a dark-coloured table-cloth; you would probably not be able to see them at a little distance. Now, gather them together in a heap, and you see them at once. The heap of shot in some ways resembles a drop of water, for in a drop of water the tiny particles (or molecules) of which it is composed are close together; but by heating water you cause them to fly asunder and scatter themselves in various directions. They are lost to sight, and moreover have no power of attracting each other or of acting in concert; each one then takes its own course, whereas in the drop of water they were in some wonderful way bound together by mutual attraction. They dance in groups; but the rude force of heat will scatter these little dancing groups, and break them up into that state which we call a state of vapour.

The forces of heat and cohesion are directly at variance; and it is just a question of degree whether the one or the other gets the mastery in this "tug of war." The more you heat the water, the faster the little groups of molecules break up and disappear in the air. They must in some way go moving between the particles of air, and collisions keep taking place with inconceivable rapidity.

And now another question arises; namely, how much water-vapour can the air take? That depends chiefly on its temperature. Air when heated will take up a great deal of steam; and the more you heat air, the more it can take up. When air at a given temperature can take up no more, it is said to be saturated for that temperature; but if the temperature be raised, it will immediately begin to take up more. For each degree of temperature there is a certain amount of water-vapour which can be absorbed, and no more. But suppose we take some air which is already saturated and lower its temperature by giving it a sudden chill, what will happen? It will immediately give up part of its steam, or water-vapour; namely, the exact amount which it is unable to contain at the lower temperature.[8]

There are various ways in which you can test this matter for yourself. For instance, take a hand-glass, and breathe on it. You know what will happen: a film of moisture forms upon it; and you know the reason why. It is simply that the cold glass gives a chill to one's breath (which being warm is highly charged with water-vapour from the lungs), and so some of the vapour is at once condensed. Now, this serves very well to explain how mountains catch water-vapour, and condense it. They are, as it were, a cold looking-glass; and the hot breath of the plains, as it strikes their sides, receiving a sudden chill, throws down part of the vapour it contains. On the higher parts of mountain-ranges the cold is so great that the water assumes the form of snow.

CLOUDS ON BEN NEVIS

Mountains, as every one knows, are colder than the plains below. No one cares to stay very long on a mountain-top, for fear of catching cold. It may be worth while to consider why they are cold. Perhaps you answer, "Because they are so high." That is true, but not a complete answer to our question. We must look at the matter a little more closely. The earth is a warm body surrounded by space in which the cold is inconceivably intense; but just as we protect our bodies against cold with garments, so the earth is wrapped up in an atmosphere which serves more or less to keep in the heat. All warm bodies give out heat as luminous bodies give out light; but the rays of heat, unlike those of light, are quite invisible to our eyes, so that we are unaware of them. These "dark heat-rays," as they are called, do not make any impression on the retina, because our eyes are not capable of responding to them as they do to the ordinary rays of light. But there is a delicate little instrument known as the thermopile, which responds to, and so detects these invisible rays; and if our eyes were sensitive to such vibrations as these, we should see heat-rays (which like light and sound are due to vibrations) streaming from every object, just as light does from a candle-flame.

Those parts of the earth which are least covered or protected by the atmosphere lose heat most rapidly,—in the same way that on a frosty day one's fingers become cold unless covered up. Now, there is less air over mountains; and in those higher regions above the peaks what air there is, is more rarefied, and therefore less capable of stopping the heat-rays coming from the earth. Professor Tyndall has shown that water-vapour in the air has a great power of stopping dark heat-rays; and the lower regions, which contain more vapour, stop or absorb a good deal of heat which would otherwise escape into space.

Look at a map of any continent, and you will see the rivers streaming away from the mountains. All those vast quantities of water come from the atmosphere; and mountains do a large share of the work of condensing it from the state of vapour to that of water. Take the map of India, and look at the great range of the Himalayas. At their feet is the hot valley of the Ganges, which meets that of the Brahmapootra River. An immense amount of evaporation takes place from these mighty rivers, so that the air above them becomes laden with water-vapour. Farther south is the tropical Indian Ocean, from which the direct rays of the sun draw up still vaster quantities of water. And so when south winds blow over India, they are full of water-vapour; and presently they strike the flanks of the Himalayas, and at once they are chilled, and consequently part with a large amount of the vapour which they contained. This is best illustrated by the case of the southwest monsoon wind of the summer season, which sets in during the month of April, and continues to blow steadily towards the northeast till October. After leaving the Bay of Bengal, this warm wind, laden with vapour, meets ere long with the range known as the Khasi Hills, and consequently throws down a large part of its vapour in the form of rain. The rainfall here in the summer season reaches the prodigious total of five hundred inches, or about twenty times as much as falls in London during a whole year. After passing over these hills, the monsoon wind presently reaches the Himalayas; and another downpour then takes place, until by the time it reaches the wide plains of Thibet, so much water has been given up that it becomes a very dry wind instead of a moist one.

It must not be supposed, however, that the condensation effected by mountains is entirely due to this coldness. They have another simple and effective way of compelling the winds to give up rain: their sloping sides force the winds which strike them to ascend into higher regions,—wedging them up as waves run up a sloping stony bank on the seashore,—and when the winds reach higher regions of the atmosphere they must (as explained above) suffer loss of heat, or in other words, have their temperature lowered. They also expand considerably as they rise into regions where the atmospheric pressure is less; and as every gas or vapour loses heat in the act of expansion, they undergo a further cooling from this cause also.

We have now learned that the cooling process is brought about in three different ways: (1) By contact with the cold body of the mountains; (2) By giving out heat into space; (3) By expansion of the air as it reaches into the higher regions of the atmosphere. The "cloud-caps" on certain mountains and promontories are to be explained by all these causes combined.

The west coast of Great Britain illustrates the same thing on a smaller scale. There the warm waters of the Gulf Stream, travelling in a northeasterly direction straight away from the Gulf of Mexico, strike the west coast of Ireland, England, and Scotland; and as most people are aware, the mild climate of Great Britain is chiefly due to this fact. If you contrast for a moment the east and west coasts of Britain, you will see that the latter is much more rocky and mountainous than the east coast. Mountains run down nearly all our western coasts. Now, it is this elevated and rocky side of Britain which catches most of the rain. Very instructive it is to compare the annual rainfall in different parts of Britain. On Dartmoor about 86 inches of rain fall every year, while in London only about 24 inches fall annually; but then London has no range of mountains near, and is far away from the west coast. Again, while people in Ambleside have to put up with 78 inches of rain, in Norfolk they are content with the modest allowance of 24 inches or so. At a place called Quoich on the west coast of Scotland, about 117 inches fall every year. These differences are chiefly due to the different contour of the land down the west side of Britain, which is mountainous, while the east side is flat, and also to the fact that while easterly winds, which have come over the continent, are dry, our prevailing winds are from the west and southwest, and are consequently heavily laden with vapour from the Atlantic Ocean. These winds follow the direction of the Gulf Stream, driving it along before them; and in so doing they take up large quantities of vapour from its surface. When these warm winds touch our western coasts, they receive a chill, and consequently are no longer able to contain all the vapour which they bring with them, and so down comes the rain.

II. Mountains are elevated reservoirs of water in one form or another, and thus not only feed the streams and rivers, but give them force and direction as well. It is very important that the mountains should not allow the waters they collect to run away too fast. Try to think for a moment what would happen if instead of being, as it were, locked up in the form of snowfields and glaciers, the water were all in the liquid form. It would soon run away, and for months together the great river-valleys would be dry and desolate. When the rain came, there would be tremendous floods; dire destruction would be wrought in the valleys; and very soon the great rivers would dwindle down to nothing. Vegetation too would suffer seriously for want of water during the summer months; and the valleys generally would cease to be the fertile sources of life which they are at present. The earth would become for the most part like a stagnant marsh.

But in the higher mountain regions there is a beneficent process going on which averts such an evil. The precious supplies of water are stored up in the solid forms of snow and ice. Now, we all know that snow and ice take a long time to melt; and thus Nature regulates and like a prudent housewife economises her precious stores. The rivers which she feeds continually, from silent snowfields and glaciers among her mountain-peaks, are the very arteries and veins of the earth; and as the blood in our bodies is forced to circulate by pressure from the heart, so the rivers are compelled to flow by pressure from the great heart of the hills,—slow, steady, continuous pressure, not the quick pulses which the human heart sends through the body.

And again, as the blood, after circulating through the body in an infinite number of life-giving streams, returns to the heart once more on its journey, so the thousand streams which wander over the plains find their way back to the heart of the mountains, for the water is brought there in the form of vapour and clouds by the winds.

When we build water-towers, and make reservoirs on high ground to give pressure to the water in our pipes, and make it circulate everywhere,—even to the tops of our houses,—we are only taking a hint from Nature. The mountains are her water-towers, and from these strong reservoirs, which never burst, she commands her streams, forcing them along their courses in order that they may find their way to the utmost bounds of continents.

But there is another way in which mountains regulate the supply of water, and prevent it from running away too fast,—one not so effective as the freezing process, but still very useful, because it applies to the lower hills below the line of perpetual snow. This may be well illustrated by the state of some of the Scotch hills in the middle of summer or autumn, when there is little if any snow resting upon them.

Any one familiar with these hills will have noticed how full of water their sides are. Tiny threads of streams trickle slowly along everywhere; peat-beds are saturated with dark-brown water; even the grass and soil are generally more or less wet, especially under pine forests. One can generally get a cup of water somewhere, except after a long dry summer, which is exceptional. Then there is the dew forming every night. Forests with their undergrowth of soil—moss and fern—also help very considerably to check the flow of water. We have often asked ourselves when watching some swift-flowing river, "Where does all this water come from? Why does it not dry up in hot weather?" The answer came fully after we had climbed several mountains, and seen with our eyes the peat-beds among the hills, and heard the trickling of the tiny rivulets hurrying along to feed some neighbouring burn, or perhaps to run into some mountain tarn or loch, and noticed the damp, spongy state of the soil everywhere,—not to mention the little springs which here and there well up to the surface, and so contribute their share.

The rivers and streams of Scotland assume various tints of amber and dark-brown, according to the amount of rain which has recently fallen. These colours are due to organic matter from the peat. Compare Scott's description of the Greta:—

"In yellow light her currents shone,

Matching in hue the favourite gem

Of Albion's mountain diadem."

The waters of some Scotch rivers after heavy rain look as black as pitch.

Nor must we omit the lakes which abound in most mountain regions, and serve as natural reservoirs for the rivers, besides giving a wonderful charm to mountain scenery.

The largest lakes in mountainous regions are found on the courses of the rivers; and there is good reason to believe that they were formed, not by any process of subsidence, but by the same operations that carved out the valleys. In many cases they are due to the damming up of a stream. But in some countries the streams dry up during summer,—in Palestine or Sinai, where there is but little soil on the hills, and consequently hardly any vegetation. Such barren hills cannot hold the continual supplies which pour gently forth from the mountains of higher latitudes.

The Alps feed four of the principal rivers of Europe. We cannot do better than quote Professor Bonney, whose writings on the Alps are familiar to all geologists. In his "Alpine Regions of Switzerland" the following passage occurs:—

"This mass of mountains, the great highlands of Europe, is therefore of the utmost physical and geographical importance. Rising in places to a height of more than fifteen thousand feet above the sea, and covered for an extent of many thousand square miles with perpetual snow, it is the chief feeder of four of the principal rivers in Europe,—the Po, the Rhone, the Rhine, and the Danube. But for those barren fields of ice, high up among the silent crags, the seeming home of winter and death, these great arteries of life would every summer dwindle down to paltry streams, feebly wandering over stone-strewn beds. Stand, for example, on some mountain-spur, and look down on the Lombardy plain, all one rich carpet of wheat and maize, of rice and vine; the life of those myriad threads of green and gold is fed from these icy peaks, which stand out against the northern sky in such strange and solemn contrast. As it is with the Po, so it is with the Rhine and the Rhone, both of which issue from the Alps as broad, swelling streams; so, too, with the Danube, which, although it does not rise in them, yet receives from the Inn and the Drave almost all the drainage of the eastern districts."

A very little reflection will serve to convince any one how vastly important and beneficial is the slope of the mountains, and how it gives force and direction to streams and rivers. Without this force, due to universal gravitation, by which the waters seek continually lower levels, the supplies in the hills would be useless. Mere lakes on flat surfaces would not answer the purpose; and so the sources of water are elevated in order that it may pour over the world below.

No writer has given such fascinating descriptions of mountains as Mr. Ruskin; and no one has more eloquently described the functions they perform. In the fourth volume of his "Modern Painters," which every one who cares for mountains should read, we find the following beautiful passage:—

"Every fountain and river, from the inch-deep streamlet that crosses the village lane in trembling clearness, to the massy and silent march of the everlasting multitude of waters in Amazon or Ganges, owe their play and purity and power to the ordained elevations of the earth. Gentle or steep, extended or abrupt, some determined slope of the earth's surface is of course necessary before any wave can so much as overtake one sedge in its pilgrimage; and how seldom do we enough consider, as we walk beside the margins of our pleasant brooks, how beautiful and wonderful is that ordinance, of which every blade of grass that waves in their clear waters is a perpetual sign,—that the dew and rain fallen on the face of the earth shall find no resting-place; shall find, on the contrary, fixed channels traced for them from the ravines of the central crests down which they roar in sudden ranks of foam to the dark hollows beneath the banks of lowland pasture, round which they must circle slowly among the stems and beneath the leaves of the lilies; paths prepared for them by which, at some appointed rate of journey, they must evermore descend, sometimes slow, and sometimes swift, but never pausing; the daily portion of the earth they have to glide over marked for them at each successive sunrise; the place which has known them knowing them no more; and the gateways of guarding mountains opened for them in cleft and chasm, none letting them in their pilgrimage, and from afar off the great heart of the sea calling them to itself: 'Deep calleth unto deep.'"

Geologists, however, do not in these days teach that the present paths of rivers were made for them, but rather that the rivers have carved out their own valleys for themselves. The old teaching before the days of Lyell and Hutton, the founders of modern geology, was that valleys were rents in the rocks of the earth's crust formed by some wonderful convulsion of Nature, whereby they were cracked, torn asunder, and upheaved. But a careful study of rivers and their valleys for many years has shown that there is no evidence of such sudden convulsions. The world is very old indeed, and rivers have been flowing much as we see them for ages and ages. A few thousand years is to the geologist but a short space of time; and there can be no doubt that a stream can in the course of time carve out for itself a valley. The operations of Nature seem slow to us because our lives are so short, and we can see so little change even in a generation; but the effects of these changes mount up enormously when continued through a long space of time. Nature works slowly; but then she has unlimited time, and never seems in a hurry. It is like the old story of the hare and the tortoise; and the river, working on steadily and quietly for hundreds or thousands of years, accomplishes far more in the end than sudden floods or violent catastrophes of any sort.

III. Mountains suffer themselves to be slowly worn away in order that the face of the earth may be renewed; in other words, they die that we, and all created things, may live. The reader will find a full account of the methods by which these results are accomplished in chapters v. and vii., and therefore we must not anticipate this part of the subject. Let it suffice for the present to say that this destruction of the hills is brought about by the action of heat and cold, of rain and frost, of snow and ice, and the thousand streams that flow down the mountain-sides. It is with soils that we are chiefly concerned at present. Try to think for a moment of the literally vital consequences which follow from the presence of good rich soils over different parts of the earth, and ask whether it would be possible for civilised races of men to flourish and multiply as they do if it were not for the great fertile valleys and plains of the world. Mountain races are neither rich nor powerful. Man exists mainly by cultivation of the soil; and among mountains we only find here and there patches that are worthy of the labour and expenditure of capital involved in cultivation. But in the great plains, in the principal river-valleys of the world, and among the lesser hill-ranges it is different. The lowlands are the fertile regions. All great and powerful nations of the world are children of the plains. It was so in the past; it will be so in the future, unless men learn to feed on something else than corn, milk, and flesh, which is not very likely.

The Egyptians, the earliest civilised race of which we have satisfactory records, dwelt in the fertile valley and delta of the Nile. They clearly perceived the value of this great river to themselves, and worshipped it accordingly. They knew nothing of its source in the far-away lakes of Central Africa; but they knew truly, as Herodotus tells us, that Egypt was "the gift of the Nile," for the alluvial soil of its delta has been formed by the yearly floods of that great river, as its waters, laden with a fine rich mud, spread over its banks, and for a time filled the valley with one sheet of water. The Assyrians and Babylonians had their home in the valley of the Euphrates and Tigris. The Chinese, too, have their great rivers. Russia is well watered by powerful rivers. The most populous parts of the United States of America are watered by the great Mississippi, and the other rivers which flow into it. England, Germany, and France are furnished with well-watered plains.

Soils are the chief form of national wealth. Minerals, such as coal and iron, are of course extremely valuable, and help to make an industrious race rich; but the land is the main thing, after all, and by land we mean soil. The two words are almost synonymous. But since the soil is formed chiefly of débris brought from the mountains, it would be more true to say that these are the real sources of wealth. Soils contain besides a large amount of valuable organic matter (that is, decayed matter which has once had animal or vegetable life) different kinds of minerals, which are necessary to the support of plant life: potash, soda, carbonate of lime, silica, magnesia, iron, phosphorus, and manganese in their various compounds are all present in the rocks of which mountains are composed. We must again fall back upon "Modern Painters" for an effective description of the forming of soil by destruction of the hills:—

"The higher mountains suffer their summits to be broken into fragments and to be cast down in sheets of massy rock, full, as we shall presently see, of every substance necessary for the nourishment of plants; these fallen fragments are again broken by frost, and ground by torrents into various conditions of sand and clay,—materials which are distributed perpetually by the streams farther and farther from the mountain's base. Every shower that swells the rivulets enables their waters to carry certain portions of earth into new positions, and exposes new banks of ground to be moved in their turn.... The process is continued more gently, but not less effectively, over all the surface of the lower undulating country; and each filtering thread of summer rain which trickles through the short turf of the uplands is bearing its own appointed burden of earth down on some new natural garden in the dingles beneath."

It may be laid down as a simple economic truth, that no nation can be powerful, rich, or prosperous, unless it possess in the first place a good soil. Other conditions, such as large navigable rivers, a good seaboard for harbouring ships, are also important; but unless the land will yield plenty of food, the population cannot be very great, for people must be fed. Foreign supplies of corn at a low price, meat and provisions of various kinds, supplement what is grown in England; but without a good soil we could not have become a powerful nation.

A high state of civilisation is in a large measure to be traced to climate and soil. The sequence is somewhat as follows:—

Mountains collect rain.

Rain fills the rivers.

Rivers make rich alluvial plains.

Agriculture follows; and food is produced.

Abundant food maintains a large population.

The population works to supply its various wants; such as roads, railways, ships, houses, machinery, etc. Then follows exchange with other countries. They send us what they can best produce, and we send them what we can best and most easily produce, and so both parties gain.

Thus towns spring up. Education, refinement, learning, and the higher arts follow from the active life of towns, where more brain-work is required, and the standard of life is higher.

And thus we may, in imagination, follow step by step the various stages by which the highest phases of civilisation are brought to pass, beginning at the mountains and ending with human beings of the highest type,—the philosopher, artist, poet, or statesman, not omitting the gentler sex, who are often said to rule the world.

The following lines of Milton possess, in the light of these facts, a deeper meaning than the poet probably intended to convey:—

"Straight mine eye hath caught new pleasures

Whilst the landscape round it measures:

Russet lawns and fallows grey,

Where the nibbling flocks do stray;

Mountains on whose barren breast

The labouring clouds do often rest;

Meadows trim with daisies pied,

Shallow brooks and rivers wide;

Flowers and battlements it sees

Bosomed high in tufted trees,—

Where perhaps some beauty lies,

The cynosure of neighbouring eyes."

With a little rearrangement of the lines, the sequence we have indicated above would be well illustrated. The mountains must come first; then the clouds, ready to bring forth their rain; then the brooks and rivers, then "russet lawns and fallows grey,"—with their "nibbling flocks." Then come the human elements in the scene,—the "towers and battlements," containing armed warriors, well fed, no doubt, and ready to do their master's bidding; lastly, the lady who adorns the home of her lord, and, let us hope, makes it worth fighting for.

For commercial purposes, large navigable rivers are of great use. And in spite of the modern railway, rivers still exert an influence in determining the routes followed by trade. London, Liverpool, Glasgow, and other busy centres of life owe their importance to the rivers which flow through them, especially since they are tidal rivers. Heavily laden barges may be seen from London Bridge going up and down with the tide every day.

Since the direction as well as the existence of large rivers is regulated by mountains, it is clear that mountains have a very direct influence on the trade of the world.

Mountains supply many of our wants. Besides water and soil, how many useful things come from the hills! Their slopes, watered by the clouds, frequently support an abundant growth of pine forest; and thus we get wood for the shipwright and joiner. Again, mountains are composed of harder rocks than we find in the plains, and that is one reason why they stand out high above the rest of the world. Their substance has been hardened to withstand for a longer time the destruction to which all rocks are subjected. They have been greatly compressed and generally more or less hardened by subterranean heat. We bake clay and make it into hard bricks; so Nature has baked and otherwise hardened the once soft strata of which mountains are chiefly composed, converting them into slates, schist, gneiss, and other kinds of rock called "metamorphic" by geologists, because they have been altered or metamorphosed from their original condition (see chapter viii., page 277). Again, granite, basalt, and other rocks known as "igneous," which once existed in a molten condition, have forced their way up from subterranean regions into the rocks forming mountain-chains; and a good deal of the hardening just alluded to is due to the presence of these fiery intruders, which have baked and hardened the rocks around them to a considerable extent, altering at the same time their mineral composition. The same causes which led to the injection of granite, basalt, and other igneous rocks in mountain-ranges brought other consequences in their train. Whatever the causes, they were closely connected with volcanic eruptions, so that highly heated water and steam found their way through cracks and other fissures in the rocks; and in the course of time the chemical actions thus set up led to the deposition of valuable metallic ores within these fissures. In this way mineral veins were formed; and volcanic action seems to be largely responsible for the production of minerals. Thus we find around Vesuvius, and in fact in all volcanic regions, large and varied supplies of minerals. Now, the geologist discovers that many mountain-chains—such, for example, as the Grampians, Alps, and Carpathians—have in past geological periods been the seats of volcanic action on a grand scale; and so we need not be surprised to learn that mountainous countries yield large supplies of valuable gems and metallic ores (see chapter viii., page 277). Even in the days of Solomon, the active and business-like Phœnicians were carrying on trade with Great Britain; and the tin came from Cornwall. Besides tin, gold, silver, lead, copper, zinc, and other metals come from our hills. Now, however, we get our copper mostly from the Andes, and our gold from Australia or South Africa, because it can be got more cheaply from these countries, to which many of our Cornish miners have emigrated.

Precious stones also come chiefly from the hills, for the same reason; for they were formed at the same time and by the same causes. Cairngorms, agates, chalcedony, jasper, onyx, topaz, diamonds, and many other gems are silent but certain witnesses to the action of subterranean heat, acting long ago on the rocks which we now see standing up high above the general surface of the ground, though once they were buried deep down below the surface. Diamonds as well as gold are often got from the beds of streams, but this is easily accounted for; the streams have washed them out and brought them down from the hills.

The following words from the Book of Job (xxviii. 5) might well be applied to the hills.

"As for the earth, out of it cometh bread:

And underneath it is turned up as it were by fire.

The stones thereof are the place of sapphires,

And it hath dust of gold."

We have thus explained the three principal services rendered by mountains, but some others remain to be mentioned.

Mountains have an important influence on climate. The climate of highlands everywhere has certain peculiarities which distinguish it from that of adjacent lowlands. The air resting on mountains is less dense than that of the lowlands, and hence has fewer molecules to obstruct the entering sunbeams by day, or to stop the outward radiation at night. Therefore mountain air must be cooler; and so we find that on mountains the mean, or average, annual temperature is lower. This rarity of the air causes the ground to become hotter by day and colder by night than the ground of the plains; and so the extremes of temperature are greater. These extremes are injurious to vegetation in the higher regions, and the want of moisture still more so. But mountain-slopes up to a certain height usually have a moist climate; that is, they have more clouds and rain than the surrounding lowlands. Below the region of snow there is generally a heavy growth of forest; and forests in their turn exercise an important influence, helping to collect moisture, and in various ways to prevent extremes either of heat or cold.

The earth is divided into three well-marked zones or belts of climate: (1) The torrid zone within the tropics, where the sun is vertical twice a year, and days and nights are nearly equal; (2) The temperate zones, where the sun's rays come more obliquely, and so are less powerful, and where the length of day and night varies considerably; and (3) The frigid zones, round each of the poles, regions of intense cold, where for six months of the year the sun is never seen. Now, these broad divisions, so familiar to school children, are considerably interfered with by the height of various districts above the sea-level, or, as geographers say, by altitude. High ranges of mountains bring somewhat arctic conditions with them, even in low latitudes, where one would expect great heat. Thus the climate of the plains is very different from that of their neighbouring mountain-ranges, although their latitudes are practically the same. Travellers in Switzerland know how hot it can be in the Rhone Valley or in the plain of Lombardy, and how much cooler it is when you get up among the glaciers and the snowfields. Or to take an illustration from Great Britain: a hot summer would be somewhat trying in Edinburgh, Glasgow, or even Inverness, because they lie low, while among the Grampians, on Speyside, or Braemar, it would be very pleasant.

Vegetation follows climate. The sultry plains of the Ganges show a luxuriant tropical vegetation, while on the middle slopes of the Himalayas the climate is temperate, like that of Europe, and consequently the vegetation resembles that of a temperate region; and the highest parts of this great range are like polar latitudes in their climate, and partly also in their vegetation.

The arctic character of the climate of high mountain regions shows itself in the flora; for on the High Alps and the Highlands of Scotland and Norway, we find no small number of truly arctic plants whose home is much farther north. A very long time ago, when the climate of the whole of Northern Europe was extremely severe, and when great glaciers descended from the mountains into the plains, so that the aspect of the country was somewhat similar to that of Greenland at the present day, arctic plants and animals came down from their northern home, and flourished abundantly. This was during the Great Ice Age, which has left behind unmistakable evidences which the geologist can interpret as if they were written records. Then for some reason the climate became milder, the glaciers melted away, in Great Britain at least; but these arctic plants were left behind, and flourished still on the cool mountains, though they died out on the warm plains (see chap. iv., pp. 123-124).

SNOW ON THE HIGH ALPS. FROM A PHOTOGRAPH BY MR. DONKIN

Mountains help to cause movement and change in the atmosphere. Let us see how this takes place. Mountains expose on one side their masses of rock to the full heat of the sun. Rocks are capable of becoming highly heated under a blazing sun: we have known stone walls, even in England, to be almost too hot to touch; and perhaps the reader may have often noticed the quivering of the hot air as it rises from the ground on a summer day, especially over a road or any piece of bare rocky ground. This quivering tells us that the air is highly heated by the ground beneath, and is consequently rising. You know how the pebbles look beneath a clear running stream; and the things which we see through air in this state all seem to be similarly moving or quivering. It is easy then to imagine how masses of heated air would rise up from the side of a mountain-range which faces the sun,—that is, the southern side,—while on the other, or northern side they cast a soft shadow for leagues over the plains at their feet. In this way mountains divide a district into two different climates, with a light warm air on their southern slopes, and colder air on the northern, and the rising of the warm air will cause a certain amount of circulation and movement. Hence mountains help to make currents in the atmosphere, and these currents produce important consequences.

When mountain-ranges trend more or less directly across the direction of prevailing winds, they always have a moist side and a dry one. In the torrid zone, where easterly winds prevail, the eastern slope is usually the moist side; but in higher latitudes, as, for example, in Europe, the western side of mountain-ranges receives the greatest amount of rainfall, because westerly winds prevail there.

Mountains are barriers dividing not only one nation from another, but separating also various tribes of plants and animals. It will be readily understood that with the exception of birds, whose powers of flight render them independent of physical barriers, most animals find mountains more impassable than men do. We can make roads and railways, but they cannot thus aid their powers of locomotion; hence mountains put limits to their migrations. Still, climate and food supplies have a greater influence in determining the boundaries of zoölogical provinces (see chapter iv.).

Mountains are the backbones of continents. A glance at a map of the world will show that there is evidently a close connection between continents and great mountain-chains. This connection shows itself both in the shapes and general direction of continents. Thus, the long continuous line of mountain-chain which extends from the southern spur of the Andes to the northern end of the Rocky Mountains,—a distance of about nine thousand miles,—corresponds with the general trend of the North American continent, and forms the axis or backbone of that vast tract of land. It seems as if the sea on its western side were kept at bay by this great rocky wall, while on its eastern side the rivers have formed new land. A line of mountains is often the coast line, for the sea cannot overcome it unless subsidence takes place. The backbone of Asia and Europe runs east and west, and the continental area of the Old World follows the same general direction.

These are the chief uses of mountains, and the facts which we have brought forward will serve to show how indispensable they are. The following eloquent passage from "Modern Painters" may form a fitting close to the present chapter:—

"And thus those desolate and threatening ranges which in nearly all ages of the world men have looked upon with aversion or with horror, and shrunk back from as if they were haunted by perpetual images of death, are in reality sources of life and happiness, far fuller and more beneficent than all the bright fruitfulness of the plain. The valleys only feed; the mountains feed and guard and strengthen us. We take our ideas of fearfulness and sublimity alternately from the mountains and the sea; but we associate them unjustly. The sea-wave, with all its beneficence, is yet devouring and terrible; but the silent wave of the blue mountain is lifted towards heaven in a stillness of perpetual mercy; and the one surge, unfathomable in its darkness, the other unshaken in its faithfulness, for ever bear the seal of their appointed symbolism:—

"'Thy righteousness is like the great mountains,

Thy judgements are a great deep.'"

CHAPTER III.
SUNSHINE AND STORM ON THE MOUNTAINS.

I would entreat your company
To see the wonders of the world.

Two Gentlemen of Verona.

"The spirit of the hills is action, that of the lowlands repose."[9] The plains, with their peaceful meadows and meandering streams, might almost be said to be asleep; but the mountains are wide awake. They are emphatically scenes of violent or rapid action. The wind blows more fiercely among the mountain-peaks than over the plains below; heat and cold are more extreme; and every process of change or decay seems quickened.

Avalanches, falls of rock, earthquakes, storms, and floods exhibit the more terrible aspects of the hills. Yet they have their gentler moods: witness the brightness of the starry sky overhead, and its intense blue by day, the wonderful sunrises and sunsets, the lovely effects of light and shade, of cloud and mist, the stillness and silence of the eternal snows in summer, and the beauty of the Alpine flower.

Let us see what those who know mountains best have to say about the wonderful things they have seen there. To begin with sunset and sunrise. Professor Bonney remarks,—

"Not the least interesting peculiarity of an Alpine sunset is the frequency with which its most beautiful effects are revealed quite unexpectedly. Often at the close of a rainy afternoon, the clouds, just before the sun goes down, break, roll up, sometimes disperse as if by magic, in the glory of those crimson rays that come darting upon them and piercing every rift. Many a time have I watched the vapours around a mountain-peak curling lightly upwards, and melting away into the sky, till at last the unclouded summit glowed with flushes of orange and rose, ere it grew pale and dead in its shroud of fresh-fallen snow."[10]

Here is a description by Professor Tyndall of a sunset witnessed in the neighbourhood of the Weisshorn:—

"As the day approached its end, the scene assumed the most sublime aspect. All the lower portions of the mountains were deeply shaded, while the loftiest peaks, ranged upon a semicircle, were fully exposed to the sinking sun. They seemed pyramids of solid fire; while here and there long stretches of crimson light drawn over the higher snowfields linked the glorified summits together. An intensely illuminated geranium flower seems to swim in its own colour, which apparently surrounds the petals like a layer, and defeats by its lustre any attempt of the eye to seize upon the sharp outline of the leaves. A similar effect has been observed upon the mountains; the glory did not seem to come from them alone, but seemed also effluent from the air around them. This gave them a certain buoyancy which suggested entire detachment from the earth. They swam in splendour which intoxicated the soul; and I will not now repeat in my moments of soberness the extravagant analogies which ran through my brain. As the evening advanced, the eastern heavens low down assumed a deep purple hue, above which, and blended with it by infinitesimal gradations, was a belt of red, and over this again zones of orange and violet. I walked round the corner of the mountain at sunset, and found the western sky glowing with a more transparent crimson than that which overspread the east. The crown of the Weisshorn was embedded in this magnificent light. After sunset the purple of the east changed to a deep neutral tint; and against the faded red which spread above it, the sun-forsaken mountains laid their cold and ghostly heads. The ruddy colour vanished more and more; the stars strengthened in lustre, until finally the moon and they held undisputed possession of the blue-grey sky."[11]

Marvellous sunsets are to be witnessed from the mountains of the New World. The following is a short and graphic description of sunset glories on the Sierra Nevada Mountains by Mr. Clarence King, whose name is well known to geologists:—

"While I looked, the sun descended, shadows climbed the Sierras, casting a gloom over foothill and pine, until at last only the snow summits, reflecting the evening light, glowed like red lamps along the mountain-wall for hundreds of miles. The rest of the Sierra became invisible. The snow burned for a moment in the violet sky, and at last went out."

These marvellous effects appeal powerfully to our sense of beauty and produce in most minds feelings of intense delight; but they also appeal to the reasoning faculty in man, and an intelligent observer naturally inquires, "Why are these things so? How are those glorious colours of crimson, orange, and yellow produced?" A full explanation cannot be attempted here; but this much may perhaps be said without tiring the patience of the reader. White light, such as sunlight or the light from an electric arc, is composed of all the colours of the rainbow,—violet, indigo, blue, green, yellow, orange, and red. A ray of sunlight on passing through a prism is split up into all these colours in the above order, and we get them arranged in a band which is known as the spectrum. Thus it is proved that white light is made up of all colours (black is not a colour, but the absence of colour). Now, when the sun is low down in the sky, as at sunset, only some of these colour-rays are able to pass through the atmosphere and so to reach our eyes, while others are stopped in passing through very many miles of atmosphere (as they must obviously do when the sun is low). Those which are stopped are the blue rays and others allied to blue, such as purple and green; but the red and yellow rays are able to pass on till they come to us. Hence red, yellow, and orange are the prevailing sunset tints.

What, then, becomes of the missing blue rays? They are caught by the myriads of little floating particles in the air, and reflected away from us. That is why we do not see them; their course is turned back, just as waves breaking against a stone sea-wall are turned back or reflected. A person situated behind such a wall will not see the waves which break against it; but suppose a very big wave came: it would come right over, and then we should soon become aware of its presence. So it is with the little waves of light: some are stopped and turned back as they break against the myriads of little dust particles and the still more numerous particles of mist always floating in the air; while others, which are larger, break over them and travel on undisturbed until they reach our eyes. Now, the larger waves of light are the red waves, while the smaller ones are the blue waves; hence there is no difficulty in understanding why the red waves (or vibrations) are seen at sunset and sunrise, to the exclusion of the blue waves. But it must be borne in mind that light-waves are of infinitesimal smallness, thousands and thousands of them going to make up an inch. Sound also travels in waves, and the phenomena of sound serve to illustrate those of light; but sound-waves are very much larger.

The reason why the sky overhead appears blue is that we see the blue rays reflected down to the earth from myriads of tiny dust and water particles, while the red rays pass on over our heads, which is just the reverse of what happens at sunset.

On the southern slopes of the Alps the blues of the sky are generally very different from those on the northern side; and this is probably due to the greater quantity of water-vapour in the air, for the moist winds come from the south. Sunrises in the Alps are quite as glorious to behold as sunsets; but comparatively few people rise early enough to see them. Speaking generally, it may be said that in Alpine sunrises the prevailing colours are orange and gold, in sunsets crimson or violet-pink. After a cool night the atmospheric conditions will obviously be different from those which exist after a warm day, and more water-vapour will have been condensed into mist or cloud. Hence we should expect a somewhat different effect.

The snowfields on high ranges of mountains are of a dazzling whiteness; and their bright glare is so great as to distress the eyes of those who walk over them without blue glasses, and even to cause inflammation. At these heights the traveller is not only exposed to the direct rays of the sun, untempered save for a thin veil of rarefied air, but also to an intense glare produced by the little snow-crystals which scatter around the beams of light falling upon them. Scientific men, who have studied these matters, say that the scorching of the skin and "sun-burning" experienced by Alpine travellers is not caused, as might be supposed, by the heat of the sun, but by the rays of light darting and flashing on all sides from myriads of tiny snow-crystals.

Occasionally a soft lambent glow has been observed on snowfields at night. This is a very curious phenomenon, to which the name of "phosphorescence" has, rightly or wrongly, been given. A pale light may often be seen on the sea during a summer night, when the water is disturbed in any way; and if one is rowing in a boat, the oars seem glowing with a faint and beautiful light. It is well known that this is caused by myriads of little light-producing animalcules in the sea-water. But we can hardly suppose that the glow above referred to is produced by a similar cause. One observer says the glow is "something like that produced by the flame of naphtha;" and he goes on to say that at every step "an illuminated circle or nimbus about two inches in breadth surrounded our feet, and we seemed to be ploughing our way through fields of light, and raising clods of it, if I may be allowed the expression, in our progress." Another observer, also an Alpine traveller, says that at almost every footstep the snowy particles, which his companion in front lifted with his feet from the freshly fallen snow, fell in little luminous showers. The exact cause which produces this strange effect at night has not been ascertained.

There is another curious phenomenon often seen just before sunset on a mountain in Hungary. It is known as "The Spectre of the Brocken." The Brocken is the highest summit of the Hartz Mountains. As you step out upon the plateau upon the top of the hill, your shadow, grim and gigantic, is apparently flung right out against the eastern sky, where it flits from place to place, following your every movement. The explanation is simply this: to the east of the Hartz Mountains there is always a very dense and hazy atmosphere, so dense that it presents a surface capable of receiving the impression of a shadow, and of retaining it, as a wall does. The shadows are really close at hand, not a long way off, as might at first sight be supposed. If very far away, they would be too faint to be visible.

In all mountainous regions the permanent habitations of men cease at a limit far below the most elevated points reached by the mountain-climber. St. Veran and Gargl, the highest villages of France and Germany, are situated at the respective heights of 6,591 and 6,197 feet; but the Hospice of St. Bernard, in Switzerland, built centuries ago to shelter travellers when benumbed with the cold, is much more elevated, its height being 8,110 feet above sea-level. The most elevated cluster of houses in the world is the convent of Hanle, inhabited by twenty Thibetan priests; its height is 14,976 feet. None of the villages of the Andes, except perhaps that of Santa Anna, in Bolivia, have been built at so great a height.

Travellers who venture to ascend lofty mountains not only have to suffer all the rigours of cold and run the risk of being frozen on their route, but they may also experience painful sensations owing to the rarefaction of the air. It would naturally be supposed that at an elevation at which the pressure of the atmosphere is reduced to one half, or even to one fourth that of the plains below, a certain uneasiness should be caused by the change, the more so since other conditions, such as warmth and moisture, are different. Undaunted climbers, like Professor Tyndall, who have never felt the effect of this "mountain-sickness" (mal de montagne), deny that the sensations proceed from anything else than mere fatigue. In the Himalayas, the traveller does not begin to suffer from the attacks of this ailment until he has reached a height of 16,500 feet; while on the Andes a large number of persons are affected by it at an altitude of 10,700 feet. In the South American mountains, the symptoms are much more serious: to the fatigue, head-ache, and want of breath are added giddiness, sometimes fainting-fits, and bleeding from lips, gums, and eyelids. The aeronaut, however, who is spared all the fatigue of climbing, rarely suffers any inconvenience except from cold, at such elevations. But on rising to greater heights, 30,000 or 40,000 feet, the malady shows itself; and if the balloon continued to rise, the aerial voyager would infallibly perish.

Professor Bonney says:—

"I have occasionally seen persons singularly affected on high mountains; and as the barometer stands at about sixteen inches on Mont Blanc, and at thirty at sea-level, one would expect this great difference to be felt. Still, I do not think it easy to separate the inconveniences due to atmosphere from those caused by unwonted fatigue, and am inclined to attribute most of them to the latter."

But the fact that the aeronaut suffers seems conclusive.

The violent storms which break upon mountain districts often cause floods of considerable magnitude, such as may be compared with the memorable bursting of the Holmfirth reservoir. Hardly a year passes without considerable damage being done: bridges are swept away; roads are buried under torrents of mud, and fields overwhelmed with débris. In August of the year 1860 a severe storm was witnessed by visitors staying at Zermatt. It began with a thunder-storm; and rain fell for about thirty-six hours, after which, as may be supposed, the torrents were swollen far beyond their usual size. Lower down in the valleys much harm was done, but there one bridge only was swept away. It was, however, an awful sight to see the Visp roaring under one of the bridges that remained, and to hear the heavy thuds of the boulders that were being hurried on and dashed against one another by the torrent.

In September, 1556, the town of Locarno, in the Canton Ticino, was visited by a destructive storm and flood. The day began by several shocks of earthquake, followed, about five o'clock, by a terrific gale from the south. Part of the old castle was blown down; the doors of St. Victor's Church were burst open by a blast while the priest was at the altar; and everything within was overturned. At midday the clouds were so thick that it was almost as dark as night. A violent thunder-storm and torrents of rain followed, lasting from two to six o'clock in the evening. The rivulets all became torrents; the stream flowing through the town was so choked by uprooted trees and rocks that its water flooded the streets and almost buried them under mud and gravel. Such a sight as this gives one a powerful impression of the geological work of streams when greatly swollen; for all this débris must have been brought down from the surrounding mountains. Many lives were lost by this calamity, and a great deal of property was destroyed. Late in the year, during unsettled weather, the traveller often encounters on Alpine passes a sudden storm of snow, accompanied by violent gusts of wind, which fill the air with drifted flakes; so that becoming bewildered, he loses his way, and at last sinks down benumbed with cold and dies. Many a frequented pass in Switzerland has been the scene of death from this cause. Exhausted with fatigue, and overcome with cold, the traveller sinks down by the wayside, and the guides, after having in vain endeavoured to urge him on, are compelled, in order to save their own lives, to leave him to his fate and press forward. The name "Tourmente" is given to these storms.

On the tops of the highest mountains, even in very fine weather, the wind often blows with great force; and the north wind, supposed to be the mountaineer's best friend, is sometimes his enemy. It not unfrequently happens that a gale renders the passage of some exposed slope or ridge too dangerous, or the intense cold produces frost-bites, so that an expedition has to be abandoned when success is within reach, which naturally is very annoying. Professor Bonney, speaking of such a gale which he experienced in 1864, says,—

"The cold was something horrible; the wind seemed to blow not round, but through me, freezing my very marrow, and making my teeth chatter like castanets; and if I stopped for a moment, I shook as if in an ague-fit. It whisked up the small spiculæ of frozen snow, and dashed them against my face with such violence that it was hardly possible to look to windward. Thin sheets of ice as large as my hand were whirled along the surface of the glacier like paper.... When these gales are raging, the drifted snow is blown far to leeward of the peaks in long streamers like delicate cirrus-clouds; and on such occasions the mountain is said by the guides fumer sa pipe (to smoke his pipe). This Mont Blanc was doing to some purpose the day that we were upon him."

It is a curious fact that these gales are often confined to the crests of the mountains, so that the wind may be raging among the peaks while a few hundred feet lower down there is comparative calm.

The chief of the prevailing winds in the Alps is the Föhn. This is a hot blast from the south which probably comes from the African deserts. On its approach the air becomes close and stifling, the sky, at first of unusual clearness, gradually thickens to a muddy and murky hue, animals become restless and disquieted by the unnatural dryness of the hot blast which now comes sweeping over the hills. In some villages, it is said, all the fires are extinguished when this wind begins to blow, for fear lest some chance spark should fall on the dry wooden roofs and set the whole place in a blaze. Still the Föhn is not altogether an "ill wind that blows nobody any good," for under its warm touch the winter snows melt away with marvellous rapidity. In the valley of Grindelwald it causes a snow-bed two feet thick to disappear in about a couple of hours, and produces in twenty-four hours a greater effect than the sun does in fifteen days. There is a Swiss proverb which rather profanely says: "If the Föhn does not blow, the golden sun and the good God can do nothing with the snow."

In summer-time, however, the south wind is never welcome, for the vapour which it brings from the Italian plains is condensed by the snows of the Alps, and streams down in torrents of rain.

A thunder-storm is always a grand spectacle. Among mountains such storms are more frequent than on the plains, and also, as might be expected, far more magnificent, especially at night. Flashes, or rather sheets, of unutterable brilliancy light up the sky; distant chains of mountains are revealed for a moment, only to be instantly eclipsed by the pall of night. Says Professor Bonney,—

"No words can adequately express the awful grandeur of these tempests when they burst among the mountains. I have often been out in them,—in fact, far more frequently than was pleasant; but perhaps the grandest of all was one that welcomed me for the first time to Chamouni. As we entered the valley, and caught sight of the white pinnacles of the glacier des Bossons, a dark cloud came rolling up rapidly from the west. Beneath it, just where two tall peaks towered up, the sky glowed like a sheet of red-hot copper, and a lurid mist spread over the neighbouring hills, wrapping them, as it seemed, in a robe of flame. Onward rolled the cloud; the lightning began to play; down the valley rushed a squall of wind, driving the dust high in air before it, and followed by a torrent of rain. Flash succeeded flash almost incessantly,—now darting from cloud to cloud; now dividing itself into a number of separate streaks of fire, and dancing all over the sky; now streaming down upon the crags, and at times even leaping up from some lofty peak into the air. The colours were often most beautiful, and bright beyond description."

A STORM ON THE LAKE OF THUN. AFTER TURNER.

The mountain traveller, when caught in a thunder-storm, undergoes a strange experience, not unattended with danger. One observer[12] thus describes his sensations:—

"A loud peal of thunder was heard; and shortly after I observed that a strange singing sound, like that of a kettle, was issuing from my alpenstock. We halted, and finding that all the axes and stocks emitted the same sound, stuck them into the snow. The guide from the hotel now pulled off his cap, shouting that his head burned; and his hair was seen to have a similar appearance to that which it would have presented had he been on an insulated stool under a powerful electrical machine. We all of us experienced the sensation of pricking and burning in some part of the body, more especially in the head and face, my hair also standing on end in an uncomfortable but very amusing manner. The snow gave out a hissing sound, as though a heavy shower of hail were falling; the veil on the wide-awake of one of the party stood upright in the air; and on waving our hands, the singing sound issued loudly from the fingers. Whenever a peal of thunder was heard, the phenomenon ceased, to be resumed before its echoes died away. At these times we felt shocks, more or less violent, in those portions of the body which were most affected. By one of these shocks my right arm was paralysed so completely that I could neither use nor raise it for several minutes, nor indeed until it had been severely rubbed; and I suffered much pain in it at the shoulder-joint for some hours."

The successive layers of snow which fall on the mountains do not remain there for ever. Unless got rid of in some way their thickness would mount up to an enormous extent. It is reckoned that on the Alps the average yearly fall of snow is thirty-three feet. In the course of a century, therefore, the height of these mountains would be increased by 3,300 feet, which we know is not the case. Various causes prevent its accumulating, among which we may mention the powerful influence of the sun's rays, the evaporation promoted by the atmosphere, the thawing influence of rain and mist, avalanches, and lastly, which is perhaps the most important, the fact that the snow composing the snowfields, as they are called, of the high regions slowly creeps down towards the valleys, where they move along as glaciers, the ends of which are gradually melted away by the warm air surrounding them, and thus the muddy glacier-streams are originated. Few perils are more dreaded by the inhabitant of the Alps than those of the avalanches. The particular way in which each avalanche descends is varied according to the shape of the mountain, the condition of the snow, and the time of the year. Hence there are three different kinds of avalanche. First, there is the ice-avalanche. The smaller glaciers, which, in the Alps, cling to the upper slopes of the higher mountains, frequently terminate abruptly on the edge of some precipice. Thus the ice, urged on by the pressure of the masses above it, moves forward until it plunges over and falls into the abyss below. Large portions break off; and these, as they bound down the cliffs, are dashed into countless pieces, which leap from crag to crag high into the air: now the falling mass, like some swollen torrent, dashes with sullen roar through a gully, now, emerging, crashes over a precipice, or spreads itself out like a fan, as it hisses down a snow-slope. These avalanches expend their force in the higher regions, and are harmless, unless any one happens to be crossing their track at the time; but accidents from this source can generally be avoided. In the distance the avalanches look like waterfalls of the purest foam, but when approached are found to be composed of fragments of ice of every size, from one, two, or more cubic yards down to tiny little balls. In spring and summer, when the white layers, softened by the heat, are falling away every hour from the lofty summits of the Alps, the pedestrian, taking up a position on some adjacent headland, may watch these sudden cataracts dashing down into the gorges from the heights of the shining peaks. Year after year travellers seated at their ease on the grassy banks of the Wengern Alp have watched with pleasure the avalanches rolling to the base of the silvery pyramid of the Jungfrau. First, the mass of ice is seen to plunge forth like a cataract, and lose itself in the lower parts of the mountain; whirlwinds of powdered snow, like clouds of bright smoke, rise far and wide into the air; and then, when the cloud has passed away, and the region has again assumed its solemn calm, the thunder of the avalanche is suddenly heard reverberating in deep echoes in the mountain gorges, as if it were the voice of the mountain itself.

The other two kinds of avalanche are composed of snow. The dust-avalanche usually falls in winter-time, when the mountains are covered deep with fresh-fallen snow. Such masses of snow, not yet compacted into ice, rest insecurely upon the icy slopes, and hang in festoons and curtains over the peaks, or lie on smooth banks of pasture, until some accident, such as a gust of wind, breaks the spell, and the whole mass slides down into the valley below. These avalanches are accompanied by fearful blasts of wind which work dire destruction. Almost the whole village of Leukerbad was destroyed by one of these on the 14th of January, 1719, and fifty-five persons perished. In 1749, more than one hundred persons were killed in the village of Ruaras (Grisons), which during the night was overwhelmed by an avalanche. So silently were some of the houses buried that the inhabitants, on waking in the morning, could not conceive why the day did not dawn. It is said, though it seems almost incredible, that in the time of the Suabian War, in the year 1498, one of these avalanches swept four hundred soldiers over a cliff, and they all escaped without serious injury.

The army of General Macdonald, in his celebrated passage of the Splügen in December, 1800, suffered severely from these dust-avalanches. A troupe of horse was completely cut through while on the march; and thirty dragoons were precipitated into a gulf below the road, where they all perished. And again, some days afterwards, in descending a gorge, the columns were repeatedly severed by avalanches; and more than one hundred soldiers, with a number of horses and mules, were lost. On one of these occasions the drummer of a regiment was carried away; and it is said that they heard him beating his drum in the gorge below, in the hope that his comrades would come to his rescue. Help, however, was out of the question. The sounds gradually became fainter, and the poor lad must have perished in the cold.

The ground-avalanches are different from those just described, consisting of dense and almost solid masses of snow which have lain for a long time exposed to atmospheric influences. They are much heavier than the dust-avalanches, and therefore more destructive; so that the inhabitants take great pains to protect themselves from this source of danger. Thickly planted trees are the best protection against avalanches of every kind. Snow which has fallen in a wood cannot very well shift its place; and when masses of snow descend from the slopes above, they are unable to break through so strong a barrier. Small shrubs, such as rhododendrons, or even heaths and meadow-grass, are often sufficient to prevent the slipping of the snow; and therefore it is very imprudent not to allow them to grow freely on mountain-slopes. But it is still more dangerous to cut down protecting forests, or even to do so partly. This was illustrated by the case of a mountain in the Pyrenees, in the lofty valley of Neste; after it had been partially cleared of trees, a tremendous avalanche fell down in 1846, and in its fall swept away more than fifteen thousand fir-trees.

The Swiss records tell us what a terrible scourge the avalanche can be in villages which in summer-time appear such calm and happy scenes of pastoral life. M. Joanne, in the introduction to his valuable "Itinéraire de la Suisse"[13] gives a list of twelve of the most destructive avalanches that have fallen in Switzerland. In old days they seem to have been as great a source of danger as in modern times. Thus we find that in the year 1500, a caravan of six hundred persons was swept away in crossing the Great St. Bernard; three hundred were buried under an avalanche which fell from Monte Cassedra (Ticino). Another one in the year 1720, at Obergestelen, in the Rhone Valley, destroyed one hundred and twenty cottages, four hundred head of cattle, and eighty-eight persons. The bodies were buried in a large pit in the village cemetery, on the wall of which was engraved the following pathetic inscription: "O God, what sorrow!—eighty-eight in a single grave!" ("Gott, welche Trauer!—acht und achtzig in einem Grab!")

It is a curious fact that animals have a wonderful power of anticipating coming catastrophes. When human beings are unaware of danger, they are often warned by the behaviour of animals. Country people sometimes say that they can tell from the birds when the weather is about to change; and there is little doubt but that sea-gulls come inland before rough, stormy weather. But in the case of earthquakes the behaviour of birds, beasts, and even fishes is very striking. It is said that before an earthquake rats, mice, moles, lizards, and serpents frequently come out of their holes, and hasten hither and thither as if smitten with terror. At Naples, it is said that the ants quitted their underground passages some hours before the earthquake of July 26, 1805; that grasshoppers crossed the town in order to reach the coast; and that the fish approached the shore in shoals. Avalanches, it is well known, produce tremors similar to those due to slight earthquake shocks; and there are many stories in Switzerland of the behaviour of animals just before the catastrophe takes place. Berlepsch relates that a pack-horse on the Scaletta Pass, which was always most steady, became restive when an avalanche was coming; so that he was valuable to his owners in bad weather. One day, when near the summit of the pass, he suddenly stopped. They foolishly took no notice of his warning this time; but he presently darted off at full speed. In a few seconds the avalanche came and buried the whole party.

If these stories can be relied upon, it would seem that animals are either more sensitive to very slight tremors of the earth, or else that they are more on the lookout than human beings. Perhaps North American Indians have learned from animals in this respect, for they can tell of a coming enemy on the march by putting their ears to the ground and listening.

But there are worse dangers in the mountains than falls of snow and ice, for sometimes masses of rock come hurtling down, or worse still, the whole side of a mountain gives way and spreads ruin far and wide. Perpendicular or overhanging rocks, which seem securely fastened, suddenly become detached and rush headlong down the mountain-side. In their rapid fall, they raise a cloud of dust like the ashes vomited forth by a volcano; a horrible darkness is spread over a once pleasant valley; and the unfortunate inhabitants, unable to see what is taking place, are only aware of the trembling of the ground, and the crashing din of the rocks as they strike together and shatter one another in pieces. When the cloud of dust is cleared away, nothing but heaps of stones and rubbish are to be seen where pastures once grew, or the peasant ploughed his acres in peace. The stream flowing down the valley is obstructed in its course, and changed into a muddy lake; the rampart of rocks from which some débris still comes crumbling down has lost its old form; the sharpened edges point out the denuded cliff from which a large part of the mountain has broken away. In the Pyrenees, Alps, and other important ranges there are but few valleys where one cannot see the confused heaps of fallen rocks.

Many of these catastrophes, known as the "Bergfall," have been recorded; and the records tell of the fearful havoc and destruction to life and property due to this cause. In Italy the ancient Roman town of Velleja was buried, about the fourth century, by the downfall of the mountain of Rovinazzo;

and the large quantity of bones and coins that have been found proves that the fall was so sudden that the inhabitants had no time to escape.

Taurentum, another Roman town, situated, it is said, on the banks of Lake Geneva, at the base of one of the spurs of the Dent d'Oche, was completely crushed in A. D. 563 by a downfall of rocks. The sloping heap of débris thus formed may still be seen advancing like a headland into the waters of the lake. A terrible flood-wave, produced by the deluge of stones, reached the opposite shores of the lake and swept away all the inhabitants. Every town and village on the banks, from Morges to Vevay, was demolished, and they did not begin the work of rebuilding till the following century. Some say, however, that the disaster was caused by a landslip which fell from the Grammont or Derochiaz across the valley of the Rhone, just above the spot where it flows into the Lake of Geneva. Hundreds of such falls have taken place within the Alps and neighbouring mountains within historic times.

Two out of the five peaks of the Diablerets fell down, one in 1714 and the other in 1749, covering the pastures with a thick layer of stones and earth more than three hundred feet thick, and by obstructing the course of the stream of Lizerne, formed the three lakes of Derborence. In like manner the Bernina, the Dent du Midi, the Dent de Mayen, and the Righi have overspread with ruin vast tracts of cultivated land. In Switzerland the most noted Bergfalls are those from the Diablerets and the Rossberg. The former mountain is a long flattish ridge with several small peaks, overhanging very steep walls of rock on either side. These walls are composed of alternating beds of limestone and shale. Hence it is easily perceived that we have here conditions favourable for landslips, because if anything weakens one of these beds of shale the overlying mass might be inclined to break away. The fall in the year 1714, already referred to, was a very destructive one.

THE MATTERHORN. FROM A PHOTOGRAPH BY MR. DONKIN.

"For two whole days previously loud groaning had been heard to issue from the mountain, as though some imprisoned spirit were struggling to release himself, like Typhœus from under Etna; then a vast fragment of the upper part of the mountain broke suddenly away and thundered down the precipices into the valley beneath. In a few minutes fifty-five châlets, with sixteen men and many head of cattle, were buried for ever under the ruins. One remarkable escape has indeed been recorded, perhaps the most marvellous ever known. A solitary herdsman from the village of Avent occupied one of the châlets which were buried under the fallen mass. Not a trace of it remained; his friends in the valley below returned from their unsuccessful search, and mourned him as dead. He was, however, still among the living; a huge rock had fallen in such a manner as to protect the roof of his châlet, which, as is often the case, rested against a cliff. Above this, stones and earth had accumulated, and the man was buried alive. Death would soon have released him from his imprisonment, had not a little rill of water forced its way through the débris and trickled into the châlet. Supported by this and by his store of cheese, he lived three months, labouring all the while incessantly to escape. Shortly before Christmas he succeeded, after almost incredible toil, in once more looking on the light of day, which his dazzled eyes, so long accustomed to the murky darkness below, for a while could scarcely support. He hastened down to his home in Avent, and knocked at his own door; pale and haggard, he scarcely seemed a being of this world. His relations would not believe that one so long lost could yet be alive, and the door was shut in his face. He turned to a friend's house; no better welcome awaited him. Terror seized upon the village; the priest was summoned to exorcise the supposed demon; and it was not till he came that the unfortunate man could persuade them that he was no spectre, but flesh and blood."[14]

The valley is still a wild scene of desolation, owing to the enormous masses of stones of every shape and size with which its bed is filled.

In September of the year 1806, the second fall of the mountain Rossberg took place, after a wet summer. It is underlaid by beds of clay which, when water penetrates, are apt to give way. The part which fell was about three miles long and 350 yards wide and 33 yards thick. In five minutes one of the most fertile valleys in Switzerland was changed to a stony desert. Three whole villages, six churches, 120 houses, 200 stables or châlets, 225 head of cattle, and much land were buried under the ruins of the Rossberg; 484 persons lost their lives. Some remarkable escapes are recorded.

In the year 1618 the downfall of Monte Conto buried 2,400 inhabitants of the village of Pleurs, near Chiavenna. Excavation among the ruins was subsequently attempted, but a few mangled corpses and a church-bell were all that could be reached.

Geologically these phenomena, appalling as they are from the human point of view, possess a certain interest, and their effects deserve to be studied.

There is yet another danger to which dwellers in mountains are occasionally exposed; namely, the earthquake. It seems to be an established fact that earthquake shocks are more frequent in mountainous than in flat countries. The origin of these dangerous disturbances of the earth's crust has not yet been fully explained. They are probably caused in various ways; and it is very likely that the upheaval of mountain-chains is one of the causes at work. Earthquakes have for many years been carefully studied by scientific men, and some valuable discoveries have been made. Thus we find that they are more frequent in winter than summer, and also happen more often by night than by day. Day and night are like summer and winter on a small scale, and so we need not be surprised at this discovery. Some have maintained that there is a connection between earthquakes and the position of the moon; while others consider that the state of the atmosphere also exerts an influence, and that earthquakes are connected with rainy seasons, storms, etc. Earthquakes are very often due to volcanic eruptions, but this is not always the case (see chapter vi., page 199).

CHAPTER IV.
MOUNTAIN PLANTS AND ANIMALS.

The high hills are a refuge for the wild goats, and so are the stony rocks for the conies.—Psalm civ. 18.

There must be few people who have neither seen nor heard of the beauty and exquisite colours of Alpine[15] flowers. They are first seen on the fringes of the stately woods above the cultivated land; then in multitudes on the sloping pastures with which many mountain-chains are robed, brightening the verdure with innumerable colours; and higher up, where neither grass nor loose herbage can exist, among the slopes of shattered fragments which roll down from the mountain-tops,—nay, even amidst the glaciers,—they gladden the eye of the traveller and seem to plead sweetly with the spirits of destruction. Alpine plants fringe the vast hills of snow and ice of the high hills, and sometimes have scarcely time to flower and ripen a few seeds before being again covered by their snowy bed. When the season is unfavourable, numbers of them remain under the snow for more than a year; and here they safely rest, unharmed by the alternations of frost and biting winds, with moist and springlike days. They possess the great charm of endless variety of form and colour, and represent widely separated divisions of the vegetable kingdom; but they are all small and low-growing compared to their relatives grown in the plains, where the soil is richer and the climate milder. Among them are tiny orchids quite as interesting in their way as those from the tropics; liliputian trees, and a tree-like moss (Lycopodium dendroideum) branching into an erect little pyramid as if in imitation of a mountain pine; ferns that peep cautiously from narrow rocky crevices as if clinging to the rock for shelter from the cold blasts; bulbous plants, from lilies to bluebells; evergreen shrubs, perfect in leaf and blossom and fruit, yet so small that one's hat will cover them; exquisite creeping plants spreading freely along the ground, and when they creep over the brows of rocks or stones, draping them with curtains of colour as lovely as those we see in the forests; numberless minute plants scarcely larger than mosses, mantling the earth with fresh green carpets in the midst of winter; succulent plants in endless variety; and lastly the ferns, mosses, and lichens which are such an endless source of pleasure and delight to the traveller. In short, Alpine vegetation presents us with nearly every type of plant life of northern and temperate climes, chastened in tone and diminished in size.

It is not difficult to account for the small size of these plants; for in the first place we cannot expect a large or luxuriant growth where the air is cold, the soil scanty, and the light of the sun often obscured by clouds, and where the changes of temperature are rapid,—which is very unfavourable to most plants. Again, in the close struggle for existence which takes place on the plains and low tree-clad hills, the smaller forms of plant life are often overrun by trees, trailing plants, bushes, and vigorous herbs; but where these cannot find a home, owing to the severity of the winter and other causes, the little Alpine plants, covered up by snow in the winter, can thrive abundantly. And lastly, like the older and conquered races of men who have been driven to the hills (see chap. i., p. [28](#)) and find shelter there, so there are both plants and animals living in the mountains which man will not suffer to live in the plain where he grows his crops, pastures his cattle, or builds his cities. We would also venture to suggest that possibly some plants have been ousted from plains by newer and more aggressive types, which came and took their place. If so, vegetable life would afford an illustration of a process which has so often taken place in human history. This is only a speculation, but still it might be worth following up. If Alpine plants, or any considerable number of them, could be shown to belong to more ancient types, such as flourished in the later geological periods, that would afford some evidence in favour of the idea. Whether this is so or not, plant life on the mountains is almost entirely protected from the destroying hands of men with their ploughs and scythes, as well as from many grazing animals. As Mr. Ruskin quaintly says:

"The flowers which on the arable plain fell before the plough now find out for themselves unapproachable places, where year by year they gather into happier fellowship and fear no evil."

It is clear that the climate of a mountainous region determines the character of the vegetation. Now, the climate will be different in different parts of a mountain-range, and will depend upon the height above the sea and other causes.[16] Some writers upon this subject have attached too much importance to absolute height above the sea, as though this were the only cause at work. It is a very important cause, no doubt, but there are others which also have a great influence, such as the position of each locality with respect to the great mountain masses, the local conditions of exposure to the sun and protection from cold winds, or the reverse. However, in spite of local irregularities there are in the Alps certain broad zones or belts of vegetation which may be briefly described as follows:—

1. The Olive region.—This region curiously illustrates what has just been said about other causes besides height influencing the climate and vegetation. For along the southern base of the Alps, the lower slopes and the mouths of the valleys have a decidedly warmer climate than the plains of Piedmont and Lombardy. Thus, while the winter climate of Milan is colder than that of Edinburgh, the olive can ripen its fruit along the skirts

of the mountain region, and penetrates to a certain distance towards the interior of the chain along the lakes and the wider valleys of the Southern Alps. Even up the shores of the Lake of Garda, where the evergreen oak grows, the olive has become wild. The milder climate of the Borromean Islands, and some points on the shores of the Lago Maggiore, will permit many plants of the warmer temperate zone to grow; while at a distance of a few miles, and close to the shores of the same lake, but in positions exposed to the cold winds from the Alps, plants of the Alpine region grow freely, and no delicate perennials can survive the winter. The olive has been known to resist a temperature of about 16° F. (or 16° below the freezing point of water), but is generally destroyed by a less degree of cold. It can only be successfully cultivated where the winter frosts are neither long nor severe, where the mean temperature of winter does not fall below 42° F., and a heat of 75° F. during the day is continued through four or five months of the summer and autumn.

2. The Vine region.—The vine, being more tolerant of cold than the olive, can grow at a higher level; and so the next zone of vegetation in the Alps may be called "the Vine region." But to give tolerable wine it requires at the season of ripening of the grape almost as much warmth as the olive needs. Vines can grow in the deeper valleys throughout a great part of the Alpine chain, and in favourable situations up to a considerable height on their northern slopes. On the south side, although the limit of perpetual snow is lower, the vine often reaches near to the foot of the greater peaks. But the fitness of a particular spot for the production of wine depends far more on the direction of the valley and of the prevailing winds than on the height. And so it happens that in the Canton Valais, the Valley of the Arc in Savoy, and some others on the north side of the dividing range, tolerable wine is made at a higher level than in the valleys of Lombardy, whose direction allows the free passage of the keen northern blasts. It is a curious fact that in the Alps the vine often resists a winter temperature which would kill it down to the roots in the low country; and we must explain it by the protection of the deep winter snow. Along with the vine many species of wild plants, especially annuals, characteristic of the flora of the south of Europe, show themselves in the valleys of the Alps.

3. The Mountain region, or region of deciduous trees.—Many writers take the growth of corn as the characteristic of the colder temperate zone, corresponding to what has been called the mountain region of the Alps. But so many varieties, all with different requirements, are in cultivation, that it is impossible to take the growth of cereals in general as marking clearly any natural division of the surface. A more natural limit is marked by the presence of deciduous trees (trees which shed their leaves). Although the oak, beech, and ash do not exactly reach the same height, and are not

often seen growing side by side in the Alps, yet their upper limit marks pretty accurately the transition from a temperate to a colder climate that is shown by a general change in the wild, herbaceous vegetation. The lower limit of this zone is too irregular to be exactly defined, but its upper boundary is about 4,000 feet on the cold north side of the Alps, and often rises to 5,500 feet on the southern slopes, which of course get more sunshine and warmth. The climate of this region is favourable to the growth of such trees as the oak, beech, and ash, but it does not follow that we should see them there in any great numbers at the present time; for it is probable that at a very early date they were extensively destroyed for building purposes, and to clear space for meadow and pasture land, so that with the exception of the beech forests of the Austrian Alps, there is scarcely a considerable wood of deciduous trees to be seen anywhere in the chain. In many districts where the population is not too dense, the pine and Scotch fir have taken the place of the oak and beech, mainly because the young plants are not so eagerly attacked by goats, the great destroyers of trees.

4. The region of Coniferous trees.—Botanically this region is best distinguished by the prevalence of coniferous trees, forming vast forests, which if not kept down by man (and by goats) would cover the slopes of the Alps. The prevailing species are the common fir and the silver fir. In districts where granite abounds, the larch flourishes and reaches a greater size than any other tree. Less common are the Scotch fir and the arolla, or Siberian fir. In the Eastern Alps the dwarf pine becomes conspicuous, forming a distinct zone on the higher mountains above the level of other firs. The pine forests play a most important part in the natural economy of the Alps; and their preservation is a matter of very great importance to the future inhabitants. But in some places they have been considerably diminished by cutting. This has especially happened in the neighbourhood of mines; and in consequence the people of the unfrequented communes have become so alive to this that some jealousy is felt of strangers wandering among the mountains, lest they should discover metals and cause the destruction of the woods. Their fears are not unreasonable; for the forests, besides exerting a good deal of influence on rainfall and climate, form natural defences against the rush of the spring avalanches (see chapter iii., page 93). It is recorded that after the war of 1799, in which many of those near the St. Gothard Pass were destroyed, the neighbouring villages suffered terribly from this scourge. Hence the laws do not allow of timber being cut in certain forests called "Bannwalde;" and in most places the right of felling trees is strictly regulated, and the woods are under the inspection of officials.

In spots high up among the mountains, to which access is difficult, the timber is converted into charcoal, which is then brought down in sacks by horses and mules. There are two ways in which timber is conveyed down from the forest: either it is cut up into logs some five feet long, and thrown into a neighbouring torrent, which brings it down over cliff and gorge to the valley below; or else trough-like slides are constructed along the mountain-sides, down which the trunks themselves are launched.

It is this region of coniferous trees which mainly determines the manner of life of the population of the Alps. In the month of May the horned cattle, having been fed in houses during the winter (as they are in the Scotch Highlands, where the cowsheds are called "byres"), are led up to the lower pastures. The lower châlets, occupied in May and part of June, generally stand at about the upper limit of the mountain region. Towards the middle or end of June the cattle are moved up to the chief pastures, towards the upper part of the region of coniferous trees, where they usually remain for the next two or three months. But there are some available pastures still higher up, and hither some of the cattle are sent for a month or more.

5. The Alpine region.—This is the zone of vegetation extending from the upper limit of trees to where permanent masses of snow first make their appearance; so that where the trees cease, the peculiar Alpine plants begin; but we still find shrubs, such as the common rhododendron, Alpine willow, and the common juniper, which extend up to, and the latter even beyond, the level of perpetual snow. The limits of this interesting and delightful botanical region may be fixed between 6,000 and 8,000 feet above the sea, and at least 1,000 feet higher on the south slopes of the Alps, which get more sunshine. It is used to some extent for pasture; and in Piedmont it is not uncommon to find châlets at the height of 8,500 feet, and vegetation often extends freely up to 9,500 feet. Here and there, at levels below this zone, many Alpine species may be found, either transported by accident from their natural home, or finding a permanent refuge in some cool spot sheltered from the sun, and moistened by streamlets descending from the snow region. But it is chiefly here that those delightful flowers grow which make the Alps like a great flower-garden,—great anemones, white and sulphur-coloured; gentians of the deepest blue, like the sky overhead; campanulas, geums, Alpine solanellas, and forget-me-nots; asters, ox-eyed daisies, pale pink primulas, purple heartsease, edelweiss, saxifrages, yellow poppies, Alpine toad-flax, monkshood, potentilla, and others too numerous to mention. Says Professor Bonney,—

"Who cannot recall many a happy hour spent in rambling from cluster to cluster on the side of some great Alp?—the scent of sweet herbage or of sweeter daphne perfuming the invigorating air, the melody of the cattle-bells borne up from some far-off pasture, while the great blue vault of heaven above seems reflected in the gentian clusters at his feet. The love of flowers seems natural to almost every human being, however forlorn his life may have been, however far it may have missed its appointed mark. It may well be so; they at least are fresh and untainted from their Maker's hand; the cry of 'Nature red in tooth and claw' scarce breaks their calm repose. Side by side they flourish without strife; none 'letteth or hindereth another,' yet so tender and delicate, doomed to fade all too soon, a touch of sadness is ever present to give a deeper pathos to our love."

6. The Glacial region.—This comprehends all that portion of the Alps that rises above the limit of perpetual snow. But a word of explanation is necessary. The highest parts of the Alps are not covered by one continuous sheet of snow; otherwise we should never see any peaks or crags there. Some are too steep for the snow to rest upon them, and therefore remain bare at heights much greater than the so-called "limit of perpetual snow," and that limit varies considerably. Still this term has a definite meaning when rightly understood. Leaving out of account masses of snow that accumulate in hollows shaded from the sun, the "snow-line" is fairly even, so that on viewing an Alpine range from a distance, the larger patches and fields of snow on adjoining mountains, with the same aspect, are seen to maintain a pretty constant level.

ON A GLACIER.

Vegetation becomes scarce in this region, not, as commonly supposed, because Alpine plants do not here find the necessary conditions for growth, but simply for want of soil. The intense heat of the direct rays of the sun (see chapter iii., pages [76-77](76-77)) compensates for the cold of the night; and it is probable that the greater allowance of light also stimulates vegetable life.

But all the more level parts are covered with ice or snow; and the higher we ascend, the less the surface remains bare, with the exception of the projecting rocks which usually undergo rapid destruction and breaking up from the freezing of whatever water finds its way into their fissures.

Nevertheless, many species of flowering plants have been found even at the height of eleven thousand feet.

It is in this region that plants are found whose true home is in the arctic regions (see chapter ii., pages 64-65).

For the sake of those who love ferns, lycopods, and other cryptogamic or flowerless plants, a few words may be said here. Of the polypodies, the beech fern and oak fern are generally common, so is the limestone polypody in places where limestone occurs. Another species (P. alpestre) very like the lady fern grows plentifully in many places. The parsley fern, familiar to the botanist in Wales and other parts of Great Britain, is common, especially on the crystalline rocks, and ascends to above seven thousand feet. The holly fern is perhaps the most characteristic one of the higher Alps. It is abundant in almost every district from the Viso to the Tyrol, ranging from about five thousand feet to nearly eight thousand feet. The finest specimens are to be found in the limestone districts. Nestling down in little channels worn out of the rock, it shoots out great fronds, often more than eighteen inches long, which are giants compared to the stunted specimens seen on rockwork in English gardens.

Asplenium septentrionale is very common in most of the districts where crystalline rocks abound. The hart's tongue is hardly to be called a mountain fern. The common brake is confined to the lower slopes.

Cistopteris fragillis and C. dentata are common, and the more delicate C. Alpina is not rare. The noble Osmunda regalis keeps to the warmer valleys. The moonwort abounds in the upper pastures.

The club-mosses (Lycopodium), which are found in Great Britain, are common in most parts of the Alps, especially the L. selago, which grows almost up to the verge of the snows. Lower down is the delicate L. velveticum, which creeps among the damp mosses under the shade of the forest. Many of the smaller species stain with spots of crimson, orange, and purple the rocks among the snowfields and glaciers, and gain the summits of peaks more than eighteen thousand feet above the sea, reaching even to the highest rocks in the Alpine chain. For the sake of readers who are not familiar with that wonderful book, "Modern Painters," we will quote some exquisite passages on lichens and mosses, full of beautiful thoughts:—

"We have found beauty in the tree yielding fruit and in the herb yielding seed. How of the herb yielding no seed,—the fruitless, flowerless[17] lichen of the rock?

"Lichens and mosses (though these last in their luxuriance are deep and rich as herbage, yet both for the most part humblest of the green things that live),—how of these? Meek creatures!—the first mercy of the earth, veiling with trusted softness its dintless rocks, creatures full of pity, covering with strange and tender honour the scarred disgrace of ruin, laying quiet finger on the trembling stones to teach them rest. No words that I know of will say what these mosses are; none are delicate enough, none perfect enough, none rich enough. How is one to tell of the rounded bosses of furred and beaming green; the starred divisions of rubied bloom, fine-filmed, as if the Rock Spirits could spin porphyry as we do grass; the traceries of intricate silver, and fringes of amber, lustrous, arborescent, burnished through every fibre into fitful brightness and glossy traverses of silken change, yet all subdued and pensive, and framed for simplest, sweetest offices of grace? They will not be gathered, like the flowers, for chaplet or love token; but of these the wild bird will make its nest and the wearied child his pillow.

"And as the earth's first mercy, so they are its last gift to us. When all other service is vain, from plant and tree the soft mosses and grey lichen take up their watch by the headstone. The woods, the blossoms, the gift-bearing grasses, have done their parts for a time, but these do service for ever. Tree for the builder's yard—flowers for the bride's chamber—corn for the granary—moss for the grave.

"Yet as in one sense the humblest, in another they are the most honoured of the earth-children; unfading as motionless, the worm frets them not and the autumn wastes not. Strong in lowliness, they neither blanch in heat nor pine in frost. To them, slow-fingered, constant-hearted, is entrusted the weaving of the dark, eternal tapestries of the hills; to them, slow-pencilled, iris-dyed, the tender framing of their endless imagery. Sharing the stillness of the unimpassioned rock, they share also its endurance; and while the winds of departing spring scatter the white hawthorn blossom like drifted snow, and summer dims on the parched meadow the drooping of its cowslip,—gold far above, among the mountains, the silver lichen-spots rest, star-like, on the stone; and the gathering orange-stain upon the edge of yonder western peak reflects the sunsets of a thousand years."

Alpine and arctic plants are met with in Great Britain, but Scotland has a much more extensive arctic-Alpine flora than England, Wales, or Ireland, the reason being the greater altitude of its mountains. The combined flora of the United Kingdom contains only ninety-one species of arctic-Alpine plants, and of these eighty-eight—that is, all but three—are natives of Scotland. Of these three the first is a gentian (Gentiana verna), which is to be found on the hills of West Yorkshire, Durham, Westmoreland, and other parts. It comes from the Alps. The second is Lloydia serotina,—a small bulbous plant with white flowers, which is found on the hills of Carnarvonshire, in Wales. The third, well known in English gardens, is London pride (Saxifraga umbrosa), which is only to be found on the southwest Irish hills.

Of the ninety-one arctic-Alpine species, just about half are also natives of England and Wales, but only twenty-five belong to Ireland. If we examine the lists of the flora of Arctic Europe we find that all these, except about six, are found in arctic regions; and if we travel farther north till we come actually to polar regions, we find nearly fifty of these species growing there near the sea-level. The Grampian Mountains are the chief centre of the Scottish arctic-Alpine flora. The two principal localities for such flowers in that range are the Breadalbane Mountains in Perthshire, and the Cænlochan and Clova Mountains of Forfarshire. There are also a goodly number on the mountains of the Braemar district.

The history of the arctic-Alpine flora of Europe is a very interesting one. These plants, whose true home is in the arctic regions, living high up on the mountains of Europe, give unmistakable evidence of a time, very far back, when Northern Europe was overrun by glaciers and snowfields so as to resemble in appearance and in climate the Greenland of the present day. This period is known to geologists as the "Great Ice Age." The moraines of glaciers, ice-worn rock surfaces, and other unmistakable signs may be well seen in many parts of Great Britain. How long ago this took place we cannot say; but judging from the considerable changes in geography which have undoubtedly taken place since then, we must conclude that many thousands of years, perhaps two hundred thousand, have intervened between this period and the present time.

When arctic conditions prevailed over this wide area, the plants and animals which now live in arctic latitudes flourished in Great Britain; but as the climate gradually became more genial, and the snow and ice melted, the plants and animals mostly retreated to their northern home. A certain number doubtless became extinct; but others took to the highest parts of the mountains, where snow and ice abound; and there they remain to the present day, separated from their fellows, but still enjoying the kind of climate to which they have always been accustomed, and testifying to the wonderful changes which have taken place since the mammoth, whose bones are found embedded in our river-gravels, wandered over the plains of Northern Europe.

Animal Life.

The rocky fastnesses of the Alps still afford a home to some of the larger wild animals which in other parts of Europe have gradually disappeared with the advance of civilisation. During the latter part of the "Stone Age," long before history was written, when men used axes, hammers, arrow-heads, and other implements of stone, instead of bronze or iron, Switzerland was inhabited by animals which are not to be seen now. The gigantic urus (Bos primigenius), which flourished in the forests of the interior during this prehistoric human period, and gave its name to the canton of Uri, has become extinct. The marsh hog was living during the period of the Swiss lake-dwellers. These people made their houses on piles driven in near the shore, and were acquainted with the use of bronze, and therefore later than the men of the "Stone Age." The remains of these strange dwelling-places have been discovered in several places, as well as many articles of daily use. The marsh hog has disappeared; and its place is taken by the wild boar and domestic hog, which afford sport and food to the present population. But taking Switzerland as it now is, we will say a few words about the more interesting forms of animal life dwelling in the Alps, beginning with those which are highest in the animal kingdom. Chief among these is the brown bear, still occasionally found, but it is exceedingly rare, except in the Grisons and in the districts of the Tyrol and Italy bordering on the canton, where it still carries on its ravages.[18] Some also believe that it still lingers in the rocky fastnesses of the Jura Mountains, to the east of the Alps. There is properly only one species of bear in Switzerland, but the hunters generally speak of three,—the great black, the great grey, and the small brown. The second of these is merely an accidental variety of the first; but between the grey and the small brown bears there is a good deal of difference. They assert that the black bear is not only considerably larger than the brown, but is also different in its habits. It is less ferocious and prefers a vegetable diet,—feeding on herbs, corn, and vegetables, with the roots and branches of trees. It has a way of plundering bee-hives and also ants' nests; it delights in strawberries and all kinds of fruit, plundering the orchards, and even making raids on the vineyards, but always retreating before dawn. As a rule it does not attack human beings. The brown bear is much more formidable, prowling by night about the sheepfolds, and causing the sheep by their fright to fall down precipices. Goats, when alarmed, leap on the roofs of the châlets, and bleat, in order to arouse the shepherds; so that when Bruin rears himself up against the wall he often meets his death. There are many stories on record of fierce fights for life between man and bear. The bear passes the winter in a torpid state, and eats little or nothing then.

The wolf, though still lingering in several lonely parts of the Alps, is rapidly becoming rare. It is most frequent in the districts about the Engadine and in the Jura Mountains. Only in winter-time, when hard pressed by hunger, does it approach the haunts of man. It takes almost any kind of prey it can get,—foxes, hares, rats, mice, birds, lizards, frogs, and toads. Sheep and goats are its favourite prey. The wolf is an affectionate parent, and takes his turn in looking after the nurslings, which is a necessary precaution, as his friends and relations have a way of eating up the babies.

The fox is common in many parts of the Alps, but not often seen by travellers. Instead of taking the trouble to burrow, he frequently manages by various cunning devices to take possession of a badger's hole. As Tschudi quaintly observes, "He has far too much imagination and poetic sentiment to like so monotonous and laborious an occupation as burrowing." Like the wolf, the mountain fox eats whatever he can catch, even beetles, flies, and bees. Those in the valleys live more luxuriously than their relations on the mountains,—plundering bee-hives and robbing orchards. As it was in Judæa in the days of Solomon, so it is now in Switzerland among the vineyards; and a peasant might well say, "Take us the foxes, the little foxes that spoil the vineyards."

The lynx is only occasionally found in the Alps, which is fortunate for the shepherds, for they can play terrible havoc with the sheep.

Wild-cats still linger in the most unfrequented parts. Their fur is valuable, and the flesh is sometimes eaten. The badger is far from common, though rarely seen by day. It is very cunning in avoiding traps, and so is generally either dug out of its hole drawn by dogs, or pulled out by a pole with nippers or a hook at the end. Passing on to less ferocious beasts, we find the otter common along the borders of rivers and lakes. The polecat, weasel, and stoat are often too abundant for keepers of poultry. The squirrel is common enough in the forests, but varies greatly in colour. It is doubtful whether the beaver still lingers by some lonely Alpine stream. It is last mentioned in a list of Swiss mammals, published in 1817, as found, though rarely, in some lonely spots. Rabbits are common, but hares rather scarce; of these there are, as in Scotland, two varieties,—the brown hare, which is seldom found at heights greater than four thousand to five thousand feet, and the blue hare, which ranges up to nine thousand feet. The latter changes colour: its fur in summer is of a dull bluish-grey, and in winter it becomes perfectly white, and so affords a striking illustration of "protective mimicry," for with snow lying on the ground it would be very hard to see the creature.

The marmot is common in all the higher Alpine regions. These interesting little creatures are very watchful, and easily scent danger. When an intruder approaches, a sentinel marmot utters a long shrill whistle, which is often repeated two or three times, and then they all make for their burrows; but it is not easy to distinguish them from the grey rocks among which they live. The fur is a yellowish or brownish grey, with black on the head and face, and a little white on the muzzle; the tail is short and bushy with a tipping of black. They have different quarters for summer and winter. The summer burrows are in the belt of rough pasture between the upper limits of trees and the snows; towards the end of autumn they come down to the pastures which the herdsmen have just abandoned and there make their winter burrows, which are much larger than the summer ones. Like rabbits, they frequently make a bolt-hole, by which they may escape from an intruder. In winter the holes are plugged up, and the marmots, rolling themselves up in a ball, go to sleep for six months or more. Sometimes hunters dig them out; but so soundly do they sleep that, according to De Saussure, they may often be taken out, placed in the game-bag, and carried home without being aroused. They wake up about April.

The chamois, a very favourite subject with the wood-carvers, is the only member of the antelope family in Western Europe; it is found in almost every part of the Alps, but is now much rarer than it was formerly. A full-grown chamois in good condition weighs about sixty pounds. The hair is thick, and changes colour with the season, being a red yellowish-brown in summer and almost black in winter. The horns, which curve backwards, rise from the head above and between the eyes to a height which rarely exceeds seven inches. When the kid is about three months old, the horns make their appearance, and at first are not nearly as hook-shaped as they afterwards become. When full-grown, it stands at the shoulder about two feet from the ground. The hind-legs being longer than the fore-legs, its gait is awkward on level ground, but they are admirably suited for mountain climbing. When at full speed, it can check itself almost instantly, and can spring with wonderful agility. Its hoofs are not well adapted for traversing the ice, and therefore it avoids glaciers as far as possible. Having a great fear of concealed crevasses, it is very shy of venturing on the upper part of a glacier; and the tracks which it leaves in these places often show by their windings and sudden turnings that the animal has exercised great caution. And so travellers often use this as a useful clue to getting safely over a glacier. Its agility is something extraordinary. It can spring across chasms six or seven yards wide, and "with a sudden bound leap up the face of a perpendicular rock, and merely touching it with its hoofs, rebound again in an opposite direction to some higher crag, and thus escape from a spot where, without wings, egress seemed impossible. When reaching upwards on its hind-legs, the fore-legs resting on some higher spot, it is able to stretch to a considerable distance, and with a quick spring bring up its hind-quarters to a level with the rest of the body, and with all four hoofs together, stand poised on a point of rock not broader than your hand."[19] The chamois feed on various mountain herbs, and on the buds and sprouts of the rhododendron and latschen (a pine). At night they couch among the broken rocks high upon the mountains, descending at daybreak to pasture, and retreating, as the heat increases, towards their fastnesses. When winter comes, they are forced down to the higher forests, where they pick up a scanty subsistence from moss, dead leaves, and the fibrous lichen which hangs in long yellowish-grey tufts from the fir-trees and bears the name of "chamois-beard." While browsing on this, they sometimes get their horns hooked in a bough, and so, being unable to disentangle themselves, perish with hunger. The senses of hearing, smell, and sight are exceedingly acute; so that the hunter must exercise all his craft to approach the animals. Pages might be filled with the hair-breadth escapes and fearful accidents which have befallen hunters; and yet they find the pursuit so fascinating that nothing will induce them to abandon it. A young peasant told the famous De Saussure (the pioneer of Alpine explorers) that though his father and grandfather before him had met their death while out on the hunt, not even the offer of a fortune would tempt him to change his vocation. The bag which he carried with him he called his winding-sheet, because he felt sure he would never have any other. Two years afterwards he was found dead at the foot of a precipice.

The bouquetin, or steinbock, once abundant throughout the greater part of the Alps, is now confined to certain parts where it is preserved by the King of Italy. De Saussure observes that in his time they had ceased to be found near Chamouni. Its whole build is remarkably strong, giving it quite a different appearance from the slender and graceful chamois.

RED DEER. AFTER ANSDELL.

The roe, the fallow deer, and the red deer have, it is said, quite disappeared from the French and Swiss Alps, but all of them occur in the Bavarian and Austrian highlands. They frequent the forests which clothe the lower slopes, and do not often wander into the more rocky districts. The wild boar only now and then appears across the Rhine, although it is common in the Subalpine forests farther east; but we can hardly consider it a true Alpine quadruped.

Passing on to the birds which frequent the Alps, we must first notice the bearded vulture, the lämmergeier of the Germans, which once was common, but now only holds its own here and there in some lonely mountain fastness. Although preferring living prey to carrion, still in many ways it is closely allied to the true vulture. The upper part of the body is a greyish-brown hue, the under side white, tinged with reddish brown. The nest, built on a high ledge of rock, consists of straw and fern, resting on sticks, on which are placed branches lined with moss and down. It is a rare thing for the traveller to obtain a view of this monarch of the Alpine birds. Like the true vulture, its digestive powers are marvellous. According to Tschudi ("Les Alpes"), the stomach of one of these birds was found to contain five fragments of a cow's rib, a mass of matted wool and hair, and the leg of a kid perfect from the knee downwards. Another had bolted a fox's rib fifteen inches long, as well as the brush, besides a number of bones and other indigestible parts of smaller animals, which were slowly being eaten away by the gastric juice. Sheep, goats, full-grown chamois, and smaller quadrupeds are eagerly devoured by this voracious bird. It is said to be bold enough to attack a man, when it finds him asleep or climbing in any dangerous place. Tschudi, in his book on the Alps, gives several instances of young children being carried off. One of these happened in the Bernese Oberland, as follows: Two peasants, making hay upon the pastures, had taken with them their daughter Anna, a child about three years old. She quickly fell asleep on the turf near the hay châlet; so the father put his broad-brimmed hat over her face, and went to work some little way off. On his return with a load of hay the child was gone; and a brief search showed that she was nowhere near. Just at this time a peasant walking along a rough path in the glen was startled by the cry of a child, and going towards the place whence it came, saw a lämmergeier rise from a neighbouring summit and hover for some time over a precipice. On climbing thither in all haste, he found the child lying on the very brink. She was but little injured; some scratches were found on her hands and on the left arm, by which she had been seized; and she had been carried more than three quarters of a mile through the air. She lived to a good old age, and was always called the Geier-Anna, or Vulture's Annie, in memory of her escape. The particulars are inscribed in the registers of the parish of Habkeren.

The golden eagle is not uncommon in most parts of the Alps, although travellers rarely obtain a near view. It is said to be very fond of hares, chasing and capturing them very cleverly. As in Great Britain, it is accused of carrying off children; but this is at least doubtful. The kite, buzzard and falcon are occasionally seen. There are at least ten species of owls, among which is the magnificent eagle-owl. The raven is found in the lonelier glens, and is often tamed. Its thieving propensities are very amusing. Alpine birds of prey correspond very closely with British. The jackdaw is also common. It would be impossible within our short limits to give a complete list of Swiss birds, but we may mention among others the nutcracker, the jay, the white-breasted swift, the wheatear, the common black redstart, the beautiful wall-creeper, and the snow-finch, which mounts to the borders of the snow. Of game-birds we may mention the capercailze, the black grouse, and the hazel grouse, all of which are common in many of the forests. The ptarmigan haunts the stony tracts on the borders of perpetual snow. In winter it turns white, and in summer greyish-brown, though a good deal of white remains.

Pheasants and partridges cannot be said to be Alpine birds; but the Greek partridge may be so considered.

Numbers of the mountain streams and tarns contain excellent trout, and most of the larger lakes are well stocked with fish. Some of the trout of the Swiss and Italian lakes are of great size. The pike frequently weigh twelve to fifteen pounds.

Reptiles are not numerous. The common frog, which is said to be found as high as ten thousand feet above the sea, swarms in some parts of the Rhone Valley. Of true lizards, five species have been recognized. The blind-worm (which is not a snake), so common on many of our English heaths, is often met with. Among the true snakes we find the English ringed snake—quite harmless—and two adders. The common adder is found at a height of seven thousand feet above the sea.

Lower forms of life not possessing a backbone (invertebrates) abound in this region; but they are far too numerous to be considered here. Butterflies and moths are abundant; and many of those which are rare in England are common in the Alps, so that the entomologist finds a happy hunting-ground. The beautiful swallowtail and the handsome apollo, coppers, painted ladies, fritillaries, and many other Lepidoptera thrive in these regions, and are less easily frightened than at home in England.

PART II.
HOW THE MOUNTAINS WERE MADE.

CHAPTER V.
HOW THE MATERIALS WERE BROUGHT TOGETHER.

These changes in the heavens, though slow, produce

Like change on sea and land.

MILTON

Probably every mountain climber, resting for a brief space on a loose boulder, or seeking the shade of some overhanging piece of rock, has often asked himself, "How were all these rocks made?" The question must occur again and again to any intelligent person on visiting a mountain for the first time, or even on seeing a mountain-range in the distance. He may well ask his companions how these great ramparts of the earth were built up. But unless he possesses some knowledge of the science of geology, which tells of the manifold changes which in former ages have taken place on the earth, or unless, in the absence of such knowledge, he chance to meet with a geologist, his question probably remains unanswered. Such questions, however, can be very satisfactorily answered,—thanks to the labours of zealous seekers after truth, who have given the best part of their lives to studying the rocks which are found everywhere on the surface of the earth, and the changes they undergo. Geology is a truly English science; and Englishmen may well cherish gratefully the memories of its pioneers,— Hutton, Playfair, Lyell, and others, who have made the way so clear for future explorers.

The story of the hills as written on their own rocky tablets and on the very boulders lying loose on their sloping sides, and interpreted by geologists, is a long one; for it takes us far back into the dim ages of the past, and like the fashionable novel, may be divided into three parts, or volumes. To those who follow the stony science it is quite as fascinating as a modern romance, and a great deal more wonderful, thus illustrating the force of the old saying, "Truth is stranger than fiction."

The three parts of our story may be best expressed by the three following inquiries:

1.   I. How were the materials of which mountains are built up brought together and made into hard rock?

2.   How were they raised up into the elevated positions II. in which we now find them?

3.   III. How were they carved out into all their wonderful and beautiful features of crag and precipice, peaks and passes?

A mountain group, with its central peak or spire, its long ridges, steep walls, towers, buttresses, dark hollows, and carved pinnacles standing out against the sky, has well been compared to a great and stately building such as a cathedral or a temple. Mountains are indeed "a great and noble architecture, giving first shelter, comfort, and rest, but covered also with mighty sculpture and painted legend;" and to many they are Nature's shrines, where men may offer their humble praises and prayers to the great Architect who reared them for His children. We have introduced this illustration because it will help us in our inquiry. Suppose we were standing in front of some great cathedral, such as Milan, with all its marble pinnacles, or Notre Dame, with its stately towers, or the minsters of York or Durham in our own country, and trying to picture to ourselves how it was built. No one has lived long enough to watch the completion of one of these great buildings; but for all that, we know pretty well how it was made, even by watching the builder's operations for a short time, or by following, as we often may, the various stages in the construction of a small house. So it is with Nature's work. We cannot, in our little lives, witness the rearing of a great mountain-chain, or even the carving of a single hill; but we can observe for ourselves the slow and continuous operations which in the course of thousands and thousands of years produce such stupendous results. We may learn how the building operations are conducted, though the final results will only be manifested in the far-distant future.

But to return to our cathedral. If we try to picture to ourselves the long years during which it was covered with scaffolding and surrounded by a busy army of workers, we shall soon perceive that the operations may be broadly divided into three heads. First, we must inquire how the separate stones of which it is composed were brought together into one place, and we shall at once picture to ourselves groups of men working in stone-quarries,—perhaps a long way off,—busy with their crowbars and hammers, breaking off large blocks of stone, and following the natural divisions of the rock that their rough labour may be lessened; for all rocks will split more easily along certain lines than along others. Sometimes it is easier to follow the "bedding," or natural layers in which the rock was formed; at other times the "joints," or cracks subsequently formed as the rocky materials hardened and contracted in bulk, afford easier lines for the workmen to follow. Others are busily engaged in placing the stony blocks on trollies drawn by horses, that they may be borne along the roads leading from the quarry to the site of the future cathedral. And so, taking a bird's-eye view, we seem to see horses and carts slowly moving on from many a distant quarry, but all converging like the branches of a river to one main channel, and finally depositing their burdens in the stone-yard where the masons are at work. Perhaps bricks are partly employed, in which case we can easily picture to ourselves the brickyards, where some are digging out the soft clay, others moulding it into bricks with wooden moulds, while others again lay them down in rows on the ground to dry, before they are baked in the ovens. And when the bricks are ready for use, the same means of transportation are employed; and cart-loads of them are borne along the country roads until they so reach their destination.

Now, all this may be summed up in the one word "transportation;" and we shall presently inquire how the rocky matter of which the mountains are built was transported.

Secondly. We have to inquire how the bricks and stones were raised up. The analogy is not quite perfect in this case; for the mountains were raised up en bloc, not bit by bit and stone by stone, as in the case of the cathedral. Still they have been raised somehow. Analogies are seldom complete in every detail; but for all that, our illustration serves well enough, and will help us in following the various processes of mountain building. In these days, the raising of the stones is mostly effected by steam-power applied to big cranes and pulleys. In old days they used cranes and pulleys, but the ropes were pulled by hand-power. In either case the work proceeds slowly; and we can easily picture to ourselves the daily raising of the stones of which the cathedral is composed. "What were the forces at work which slowly raised the mountains?" This question we will endeavour to answer later on (see next chapter). This work may be included in the one word, "elevation."

And lastly. We must inquire how the carving of the stately building was effected, how its pinnacles received their shape, and how all those lovely details received their final forms; how the intricate traceries of its windows were made, and the statues carved which adorn its solemn portals. This question is easily answered, for we are all more or less familiar with what goes on in a stone-mason's yard. Under those wooden sheds we see a number of skilled labourers at work, busy with their chisels and mallets, cutting out, according to the patterns made from the architect's detailed drawings, the portions of tracery for windows, or the finials, crockets, and other features of the future building. In another part of the yard may be seen the stone-cutters, working in pairs and slowly pulling backwards and forwards those long saws which, with the help of water and sand, in time cut through the biggest blocks. All this work then may be summed up under the one word, "ornamentation," for it includes the cutting and carving of the stone.

Our three lines of inquiry may now be summed up in these three words, which are easily remembered:—

- Transportation,
- Elevation,
- Ornamentation.

Taking the first of these subjects for consideration in the present chapter, we have now to inquire into the nature of the materials of which mountains are composed and the means by which they have been brought together and compacted into hard rock.

First, with regard to the nature of the materials which Mother Earth uses to build her rocky ramparts: they are the same as the ordinary rocks of which the earth's crust is composed; and the greater part of them have been formed by the action of water. These are the ordinary "stratified" rocks, which in one form or another meet us almost everywhere, and may be said to be aqueous deposits, or sediments formed in seas and inland lakes. They are always arranged in layers, known to geologists as "strata," because they have been gently laid down, or strewn (Latin, stratum), at the bottom of some large body of water. There were pauses in the deposition of the materials, during which each layer had time to harden a little before the next one was formed. This accounts for the stratification. In this way great deposits of sandstone, clay, and limestone, with their numerous varieties, have been in the course of ages gradually piled up, till they have attained to enormous thickness, which at first sight seem almost incredible; but the bed of the seas in which they formed was probably undergoing a slow sinking process that kept pace with the growth of these deposits, otherwise the sea might have been more or less filled up.

And these processes are still going on. In fact, it is entirely by watching what goes on now that geologists are able to explain what took place a very long time ago when there were no human beings on the earth to record the events that took place. And so we argue from the present to the past, from the known to the unknown. In other words, geology is based upon physical geography, which tells us of the changes now in progress on the earth. Thus, sandstone, as frequently met with in different parts of Great Britain, and largely used for building purposes, such as the familiar old red sandstone[20] of South Wales, Hereford, and the north of England and different parts of Scotland, was once soft sand in no way at all different from the sand of the seashore at the present day, or of the sandy bed of the North Sea. In process of time it became hardened, and acquired its characteristic red colour, which is due to oxide of iron. In some places numerous fossil fishes have been discovered in this interesting formation, so intimately associated with the name of Hugh Miller, who first thoroughly explored it; these and other remains entombed therein tell us of the strange forms of life which flourished on the earth during that very old-fashioned period of the world's history; and by putting together all kinds of evidences derived from the rock itself, geologists are able to form a very good idea of the way in which this rock-deposit was accumulated, always, however, basing their conclusions on a thorough knowledge of what goes on at the present day in seas, rivers, and inland lakes.

In the great series of stratified rocks forming what is commonly called the crust of the earth (an unfortunate term which has survived from the time when the interior of the earth was generally believed to be in a fiery molten condition, and covered by a thin coating of solid rock at the surface), there are besides the sandstones, of which we have just spoken, great deposits of dark-coloured clays, shales, and slates. All these can be accounted for by the geologist. They are simply different states of what was once soft mud. The slates tell us that they have been subjected to very severe pressure, which squeezed their particles till they were elongated and all arranged in one direction, and this is the reason why they split up into thin sheets.

Others, again, represent vast deposits of carbonate of lime, thousands of feet thick and now occupying hundreds of square miles of the earth's surface. Limestone rocks are as abundant in our own country as the sandstones, shales, or slates. The chalk of which the North and South Downs are composed is a familiar example. It is seen again forming Salisbury Plain, in Hampshire and the Isle of Wight, and then it may be traced running up the country in a long band through the counties of Oxford, Cambridge, Lincoln, until it reaches the coast at Flamborough Head in Yorkshire. Then we have the Bath Oölites so much used in building, for they form an admirable "freestone" that can be easily carved and cut in any direction (hence the term "freestone"); and lastly, the great mountain limestone so well developed in South Wales, Yorkshire, and the Lake country. All these were slowly built up at the bottom of the seas which existed in past ages; great beds of gravel formed at the mouths of rivers, and long banks of pebbles and rounded stones collected on the shore of primeval seas, and were ground against each other as now by the action of the waves, until all their corners were rubbed off. Pebble-beds, called by geologists conglomerates, are met with among the stratified rocks; and their story is easily read by studying what takes place at the present day on our seashores.

CHALK ROCKS, FLAMBOROUGH HEAD. From a Photograph by G. W. Wilson.

Now, the sandstones, clays, gravels, and pebble-beds all represent, as will presently be explained, so much material worn away from the surface of the land and swept into the ocean (or in some cases into inland seas and lakes) by streams and rivers, which are the great transporting agents of the world. Hence such deposits of débris, supplied by the constant wear and tear of all rocks exposed to the atmosphere, are truly sedimentary and have a purely mechanical origin. But it is not so with the limestones. The latter were never transported, but grew at the bottom of the sea in very wonderful ways. They have nothing to do with the wear and tear of the land to which the others owe their existence, but represent vast quantities of carbonate of lime extracted from sea water. Sea water contains a certain amount of this substance in a dissolved state, or "in solution," as a chemist would say; and the way in which this is extracted by the agency of various creatures, such as coral polypes and little microscopic creatures that build their shells of carbonate of lime, of great beauty, forms one of the most interesting subjects presented to the student of physical geography. Hence, since limestone can only be accounted for by the agency of living organisms,[21] it is rightly termed an organic deposit, and the others are said to be mechanical deposits. But both are called "aqueous rocks," because they are formed under water. It is important to distinguish clearly between these two very different methods of rock-formation.

But although water plays such a very important part in the making of the common rocks around us, yet there are others which have quite a different origin,—rocks which have come up from below the surface of the earth in a heated and molten condition, such as the lavas that flow from volcanoes in active eruptions and the showers of ashes and fine volcanic dust which often attend such eruptions (see chap. viii., pp. 271-272). Some highly heated rocks, though they never rise to the surface to form lava-flows, are forced up with overwhelming pressure from below, and wedge themselves into the sedimentary rocks that overlie them, thus forming what are known as volcanic dykes, and intrusive masses or sheets of once molten rock. In this category we include such rocks as basalt, felstone, pitchstone, and other rocks of fiery origin that have flowed from volcanoes as lava, as well as those like granite, which have cooled and become solid below the surface, and are Plutonic, or deep-seated, igneous rocks. Granite may be exposed to the surface of the earth when the rocks which once overlaid it have been worn away or "denuded." It is frequently seen in the central regions of mountain-chains, where a vast amount of erosion has been effected. Thus we see that heat has played its part in the making of rocks; and for this reason such rocks as we have just mentioned are called igneous. Fire and water are therefore very important geological agents; but we should say heat rather than fire, because the latter word might convey a false impression. No rocks can be burned except coal, which may be considered rather as a mineral deposit than as a rock. Some rocks may be heated, and undergo many and various changes in their mineral composition; but they are not capable of combustion.

So far, then, we have learned that the rocks exposed to view on the surface of the earth may be divided into two classes; that is, aqueous and igneous. There is yet a third class, which, though of aqueous origin, has in course of time suffered considerable from the internal heat of the earth and the enormous pressure due to the weight of overlying rocks. Such rocks have been greatly changed from their original condition, both in appearance and in mineral composition, and are said to be "metamorphic," a word which implies change. Thus chalk, or other limestone rock, has been metamorphosed into marble; shales and slates into various kinds of "schists,"[22] such as mica-schist, and even into gneiss, which closely resembles granite. And it is quite possible that even granite may in some cases be the result of the melting and consolidation under great pressure of certain familiar stratified rocks. It is quite conceivable that slate might be converted into granite, for their chemical composition is similar, only the minerals of which it is composed would require to be rearranged and grouped into new compounds. This would seem quite possible; but at present we have no direct proof of such a change having taken place. Even igneous rocks are found in some places to have suffered very considerable change.

In some inland seas, like the Caspian Sea, deposits of rock salt and gypsum may be formed by chemical precipitation, owing to evaporation from the surface.

The various kinds of rock known to geologists may be conveniently arranged as follows:

Rocks of aqueous origin.	I. Sedimentary.	Clay, shale, slate, etc. Sandstones. Conglomerates.
	II. Organic.	Limestones. Flint. Coal.
	III. Chemical.	Rock salt. Gypsum, etc.
Rocks of igneous origin.	I. Volcanic	Lavas. Volcanic ashes, etc.
	II. Plutonic	Basalt. Granite.
Metamorphic rocks of aqueous and igneous origin.		Marbles. Various kinds of schists. Gneiss, etc.

So far we have only attempted to state very briefly the different kinds of rocks, and to point out that they were formed in various ways. We must now consider the question of rock-making more closely, and see what we can learn about the wonderful ways in which rocks are made; and it may be instructive to glance at the conflicting opinions on this subject which learned men held not very long ago.

At the end of the last century a great controversy took place on the question of the origin of rocks, and the learned men of the day were divided into two parties. One of these parties, following the teaching of Werner, professor of mining at Freyburg, who inspired great enthusiasm among his disciples, declared that all rocks were formed by the agency of water. This was a very sweeping and of course rash conclusion. But whenever they examined rocks, they found so many clear evidences of the action of water that a powerful impression of the importance of this agency was naturally made on their minds. They found rocks uniformly arranged in great layers which extended for long distances, and containing the remains of animals which must undoubtedly have lived in the seas or estuaries. These layers were further divided into smaller layers, such as clearly were formed by the slow settling down of sand and mud. Others again contained gravels and rounded pebbles, testifying in no uncertain way to the action of water. Even the little grains of sand are obviously water-worn. This teaching was quite sound so long as they confined their attention to clays, sandstones, and limestones; but when they came to basalt and granite, a blind adherence to the views of their master caused them to shut their eyes to the clear evidences of the action of heat, presented by such rocks. The crystalline structure of such rocks; their irregular arrangement, often so different from the uniform disposition of the stratified rocks (although it must be admitted that ancient lava-flows often lie very evenly between aqueous rocks), and the way in which they burst through overlying rocks, thus proving their former molten condition; the signs of alteration exhibited in the aqueous rocks into which they intruded themselves (changes which are obviously due to the action of heat),—these and other evidences were entirely overlooked, and Werner declared that basalt had been found as a sediment under water.

This school of geologists, believing so strongly in the all-powerful influence of Father Neptune, received the not inappropriate title of "Neptunists."

On the other hand, the party who happened to be in districts where granite, basalt, and such igneous rocks abounded were equally impressed with the importance of the powerful agency of heat. To them nearly every rock they met with seemed to show some signs of its action. And since Pluto was the classical deity of the lower regions, and the earth shows evidences in places of greater heat below the surface, this party received the title of "Plutonists;" and so the battle raged hotly for some time between the Neptunists, with their claims for cold water, and the fiery Plutonists of the rival school of Edinburgh, with their subterranean heat. Fire and water are never likely to agree; and they did not do so in this case. But now that the battle is over, and both sides are found to have been partly right and partly wrong,—though the Neptunists have the advantage,—we can afford to smile at the fierceness of the contest, and wonder how it was that each side thought they were so entirely in the right.

Let us now consider the aqueous rocks, and see if we can gain a clear idea of the ways in which they were formed; and first, we will take those of a purely sedimentary origin,—the sandstones, pebble-beds, gravels, and clays.

These, as the reader has already probably guessed, have all been transported by means of streams and rivers, and settled down quietly in seas at the mouths of rivers or in inland lakes. There is no trace of the action of heat in the forming of these rocks, though they often show signs of having suffered more or less change from contact with highly heated igneous rocks of later date which forcibly intruded themselves from below; and if the change thus effected were considerable, we should call the rocks so altered metamorphic. But we are now dealing with their original state and how they were made; and of that there is no possible doubt whatever. So for the time being we may call ourselves Neptunists.

Streams and rivers are the great transporting agents whereby the never-failing supply of débris from the waste of the land is unceasingly brought down from the mountains and hills, through the broad valleys and along the great plains, until finally it is flung into the sea. The sea is the workshop where all the sedimentary rocks are slowly manufactured from the raw material brought to it by the rivers. But for the present we must confine our attention to the question of transport. Referring back to our illustration of the cathedral, we may say that streams and rivers play the part of cart and horses. They bring the materials down from the quarry to the scene of action,—the workshop where they are wanted. The quarries, in this case, may be said to be almost everywhere. For wherever rocks and soil are exposed to the action of wind and weather, there is certain to be more or less decay and crumbling away. But it is among the hills and in the higher parts of the mountains that the forces of destruction are most active. How this is brought about will be discussed in the seventh chapter, on the carving of the hills. The frequent slopes covered with loose stones are sufficient evidence of the continual destruction that takes place in these regions.

The transporting powers of rivers are truly prodigious. Looking at a stream or river after heavy rain, we see its waters heavily laden with mud and sand; but it is difficult to realise from a casual glance the vast amount of material that is thus brought down to lower levels. If we could trace the sediment to its source, we must seek it among the rocks of mountains far away. Step by step we may trace it up along the higher courses of the river, then along mountain streams rushing over their rocky beds, tumbling in cascades over broken rocks, or leaping in waterfalls over higher projections of rock, until we come to the deep furrows on the sides of mountains along which loose fragments of rock come tumbling down with the cascades of water that run along these steep channels after heavy rain, leaving at the base of the mountain great fan-shaped heaps of stones.

"Oft both slope and hill are torn

Where wintry torrents down have borne,

And heaped upon the cumbered land

Its wreck of gravel, rocks, and sand."

These accumulations are gradually carried away by the larger mountain streams, which in hurrying them along cause a vast amount of wear and tear; so that their corners are worn off, and they get further and further reduced in size, becoming mere round pebbles lining the bed of the stream, and finally by the time they reach the large slow-moving rivers of the plains are mainly reduced to tiny specks of mud or grains of sand. So then the rivers and streams not only transport sediment, but they manufacture it as they go along. And thus they may be considered as great grinding-mills, where large pieces of stone go in at one end, and only fine sand and mud come out at the other.

The amount of land débris thus transported depends partly on the carrying power of rivers, which varies with the seasons and the annual rainfall; partly on the size of the area drained by a river; and again, partly on the nature of the rocks of which that area is composed.

A stream, moving along at the rate of about half a mile (880 yards) an hour, which is a slow, rate, can carry along ordinary sandy soil suspended in a cloud-like fashion in the water; when moving at the rate of two thirds of a mile (about 1,173 yards) an hour, it can roll fine gravel along its bed; but when the rate increases to a yard in a second, or a little more than two miles an hour, it can sweep along angular stones as large as an egg. But streams often flow much faster than this, and so do rivers when swollen by heavy rain.

A rapid torrent often flows at the rate of eighteen or twenty miles an hour, and then we may hear the stones rattling against each other as they are irresistibly rolled onward; and during very heavy floods, huge masses of rock as large as a house have been known to be moved.

These are the two principal ways in which streams and rivers act as transporting agents: they carry the finer materials in a suspended state (though partly drifting it along their beds); and they push the coarser materials, such as gravel, bodily along. But there is one other way in which they carry on the important work of transportation, which, being unseen, might easily escape our notice. Every spring is busily employed in bringing up to the surface mineral substances which the water has dissolved out of the underground rocks. This invisible material finds its way, as the springs do, to the rivers, and so finally is brought into that great reservoir, the sea. Rain and river water also dissolve a certain amount of mineral matter from rocks lying on the surface of the earth. Now, the material which is most easily dissolved is carbonate of lime. Hence if you take a small quantity of spring or river water and boil it until the whole is evaporated, you will find that it leaves behind a certain amount of deposit. This, when analysed by the chemist, proves to be chiefly carbonate of lime; but it also contains minute quantities of other minerals, such as common salt, potash, soda, oxide of iron, and silica, or flint. All these and other minerals are found to be present in sea water.

The waters of some of the great rivers of the world have been carefully examined at different times, in order to form some idea of the amount of solid matter which they contain, both dissolved and suspended; and the results are extremely important and interesting, for they enable us to form definite conclusions with regard to their capacity for transport. This subject has been investigated with great skill by eminent men of science. The problem is a very complicated one; but it is easy to see that if we know roughly the number of gallons of water annually discharged into the sea by a big river, and the average amount of solid matter contained in such a gallon of water, we have the means of calculating, by a simple process of multiplication, the amount of solid matter annually brought down to the sea by that river. But we must also add the amount of sand, gravel, and stones pushed along its bed. This may be roughly estimated and allowed for. These are some of the results:

The amount of solid matter discharged every year by that great river, the Mississippi, if piled up on a single square mile of the bed of the sea,—say, in the Gulf of Mexico, where that river discharges itself,—would make a great square-shaped pile 268 feet high. But the Gulf Stream, sweeping through this gulf, carries the materials for many and many a mile away; so that in course of time it gradually sinks and spreads itself as a fine film or layer over part of the great Atlantic Ocean. The mud brought down by the great river Amazon spreads so far into the Atlantic Ocean as to discolour the water even at a distance of three hundred miles. The Ganges and the Brahmapootra, flowing into the Bay of Bengal, discharge every year into that part of the Indian Ocean 6,368,000,000 cubic feet of solid matter. This material would in one year raise a space of fifteen square miles one foot in height. The weight of mud, etc., that these rivers bring down is sixty times that of the Great Pyramid of Egypt, or about six million tons.

Or, to put the matter in another way, if a fleet of more than eighty "Indiamen," each with a cargo of fourteen hundred tons of solid matter, sailed down every hour, night and day, for four months, and discharged their burdens into the waters of the Indian Ocean, they would only do what the mighty Ganges does quietly and easily in the four months of the flood season.

It is probable that even the Thames, a small river compared to those just mentioned, manages to bring down, in one way or another, fourteen million cubic feet of solid matter. These few figures may suffice to give the reader some idea of the enormous amount of rock-forming materials brought down to the seas at the present day.

Of course they are spread out far and wide by the numerous ocean currents, some of which flow for hundreds of miles; and so the bed of the sea can only be very slowly raised by their accumulation. Still the geologist can allow plenty of time, for there is no doubt that the world is immensely old; and if we allow thousands of years, we may easily comprehend that deposits of very considerable thickness may in this way accumulate on the floors of the oceans. Also the coasts of continents and islands suffer continual wear and tear at the hands of sea waves; and thus the supply of sediment is increased.

When the geologist comes to study the great rock-masses—hundreds, and even thousands, of feet in thickness—of which mountain-ranges are composed, he finds all those kinds of rock which we have just been considering,—sandstones, shales (or hardened clays), pebble-beds, and limestones,—and endeavours to picture to himself their gradual growth in the ways we have described. In so doing, he is driven to the conclusion that many thousands of years must have been occupied in their construction.

We must now say a few words about those other aqueous rocks which have an organic origin, of which limestone is the chief. It is indeed a startling conclusion that deposits of great thickness, and ranging for very many miles over the earth's surface, have been slowly built up through the agency of marine animals extracting carbonate of lime from the sea. Yet such is undoubtedly the case. Of this important process of rock-building coral reefs are the most familiar example. The great barrier reef along the northeast coast of Australia is about 1,250 miles long, from ten to ninety miles in width, and rises at its seaward edge from depths which in some places certainly exceed eighteen hundred feet. It may be likened to a great submarine wall. Now, all this solid masonry is the work of humble coral polypes (not "insects"), building up their own internal framework or skeleton by extracting carbonate of lime from sea water. Then the breakers dashing against coral reefs produce, by their grinding action, a great deal of fine "coral-sand" and calcareous mud, which covers the surrounding bed of the sea for many miles.

Now, geologists find that some limestone formations met with in the stratified rocks have certainly been formed in this way; for example, certain parts of the great "mountain limestone." This is proved by the fossil corals it contains, and by tracing the old coral reefs; but it is also largely formed by the remains of other graceful calcareous creatures known as encrinites, or "sea-lilies," with long branching arms that waved in the clear water. Such creatures still exist in some deeper parts of the sea, and look more like plants than animals. In former ages they existed in great abundance, and so played an important part as rock-formers,—for their stems, branches, and all are made of little plates of carbonate of lime, beautifully fitting together like the separate bones, or vertebræ, composing the backbone of a fish; and when the creatures died, these little plates no longer held together, but were scattered on the floor of the sea-bed. Shell-fish abounded too, and their shelly remains accumulated into regular shell-beds in some places. But at times mud and sand would come and cover over all these organic deposits.

But of all rocks that have an organic origin, chalk is the most interesting. Geologists were for a long time puzzled to know how this rock could have been formed; but some soundings made in the Atlantic Ocean previous to the laying of the first Atlantic cable led to a very important discovery, which at once threw a flood of light on the question. Samples of the mud lying on the bed of this ocean at considerable distances from the European and American coasts, and at depths varying from one thousand to three thousand fathoms, were brought up by sounding apparatus.

Little was it thought that the dull grey ooze covering a large part of the Atlantic bed would bring a message from the depths of the sea, and furnish the answer to a great geological problem. Yet such was the case; for under the microscope this mud was seen to be chiefly composed of very minute and very beautiful shells, now known as foraminifera, and much prized by microscopists. These tiny shells are found at or near the surface of the sea; and after the death of the creatures that inhabit them (which are only lumps of protoplasm with no organs of any kind), the shells slowly sink down to the bed of the ocean. Now, these creatures multiply at so inconceivable a rate that a continuous shower of dead shells seems to be taking place, and the result is the slow accumulation over vast areas of the Atlantic and Pacific oceans of a great deposit of calcareous ooze, which if raised above the sea-level would harden into a rock very similar to chalk.

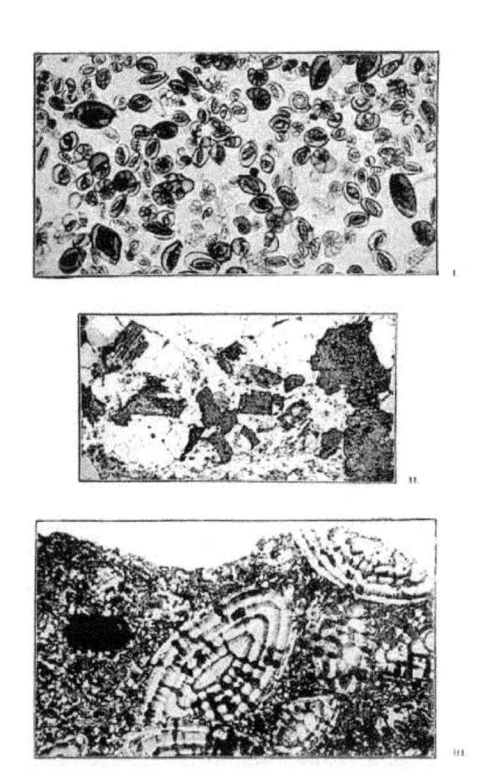

MICROPHOTOGRAPHS ILLUSTRATING ROCK FORMATION.

I. Foraminifera. II. Section of Granite. III. Nummulitic Limestone.

But this process only takes place in the deeper parts of our seas, far removed from land, where the supply of land-derived materials fails,—for even the finest mud supplied by rivers probably all settles down before travelling two or three hundred miles from its native shores.

Thus we learn that when one agency fails, Nature makes use of another to take up the important work of rock-building. How the other rocks which we mentioned in our list were formed,—such as granite, basalt, and the metamorphic rocks,—we must explain in a future chapter dealing with volcanoes and their work.

CHAPTER VI.
HOW THE MOUNTAINS WERE UPHEAVED.

The notion that the ground is naturally steadfast is an error,—an error which arises from the incapacity of our senses to appreciate any but the most palpable, and at the same time most exceptional, of its movements. The idea of terra firma belongs with the ancient belief that the earth was the centre of the universe. It is, indeed, by their mobility that the continents survive the increasing assaults of the ocean waves, and the continuous down-wearing which the rivers and glaciers bring about.—PROFESSOR SHALER.

We have found out the quarries which supplied the rocky framework of mountains, and have learned how the work of transporting these vast quantities of stone was accomplished by the agency of ever-flowing glaciers, rivers, and streams.

We must now consider the second stage of the work, and inquire how the mountains were raised up. Referring back to our illustration of the cathedral (see pages 143-147), it will be remembered that this work was included under the head of Elevation. But perhaps some one might ask: "How do you know that the mountains have been elevated or upheaved? Is it not enough to suppose that they owe their height entirely to the fact that they are composed of harder rock, and so have been more successful in resisting the universal decay and destruction?" Now, such an objection contains a good deal of truth, for mountains are formed of hard rocks; but at the same time we know that the agents of denudation are more active among them than on the plains below, so that, in the higher mountain regions at least, the work of demolition may actually proceed faster than it does on low ground.

Mountains are higher than the rest of the world, not merely because they are built of more lasting material, but also because they have been uplifted for thousands of feet above the level of the sea; and the evidence of their upheaval is so plain as to be entirely beyond doubt.

Let us inquire into the nature of this evidence. We have seen that the rocks of which mountains are composed were for the most part formed at the bottom of the sea. When the geologist finds, as he frequently does, buried in mountain rocks the fossil remains of creatures that must have lived in the sea (and often very similar to those living there now), he is compelled to think of the gigantic upheavals that must have taken place before those remains could arrive at their present elevated position.

Numerous examples might be given; but we will only mention three. In the Alps marine fossils have been detected at a height of 10,000 feet above sea-level, in the Himalayas at a height of 16,500 feet, and in the Rocky Mountains at a height of 11,000 feet.

Again we must take it for granted that all the stratified or sedimentary rocks (see pages 148-149) with some trivial exceptions, such as beds of shingle and conglomerates, have been formed in horizontal layers. This is one of the simple axioms of geology to which every one must assent.

Now, if we find in various parts of the continents, and especially among the mountains, such strata sloping or "dipping" in various directions, sometimes only slightly, but sometimes very steeply,—nay, even standing up on end,—the conclusion that they have been upheaved and pushed or squeezed into these various positions by some subsequent process is irresistible. But this is not all; for in every mountain region we find that the rocks have been crumpled, twisted, and folded in a most marvellous manner. Solid sheets of limestone may be seen, as it were, to writhe from the base to the summit of a mountain; yet they present everywhere their truncated ends to the air, and from their incompleteness it is easy to see what a vast amount of material has been worn away, leaving, as it were, mere fragments behind. The whole geological aspect of the Alps (for example) is suggestive of intense commotion; and they remain a marvellous monument of stupendous earth-throes, followed by prolonged and gigantic denudation (see diagrams, chap. ix., p. 307).

There are certain features found in all mountain-chains which must be carefully borne in mind, especially when we are considering the explanations that have been suggested with regard to their upheaval. These may be briefly stated as follows:—

1.   1. Mountain-chains tend to run in straight or gently curving lines.

2.   2. Their breadth is small compared to their length, and their height smaller still.

3.   3. They rise sharply and are clearly marked off from the country on either side.

4.   4. They form the backbones of continents.

5.   5. The rocks of which they are composed have been greatly disturbed, folded, and contorted.

6.   6. There is often a band of crystalline rocks (granite, gneiss, etc.) running along the centre of a high range.

7.   7. They are connected with lines of volcanoes.

8.   8. They are frequently affected by earthquakes.

Having arrived at the conclusion that the mountains show evident signs of upheaval, let us proceed to inquire whether any movements, either upward or downward, are taking place now on the earth, or can be proved to have done so within comparatively recent times. On this question there is ample evidence at our disposal.

More than one hundred and thirty years ago, Celsius, the Swedish astronomer, was aware, from the unanimous testimony of the inhabitants of the sea-coasts, that the Gulf of Bothnia was constantly diminishing both in depth and extent. He resorted to measurements in order to prove (as he thought) that the waters of the Baltic were changing their level. This was a mistaken idea; and we now understand that the level of the sea does not change, except under the influence of the daily rise and fall of the tide, which is easily allowed for. However, that was the idea then; and it survived for some time. But if the sea-level were continually sinking, the water, which, owing to the influence of gravitation, must always remain horizontal, would equally retreat all round the Scandinavian peninsula and on all our seashores. But this is not the case. Again, it would be impossible on this theory to explain the curious fact that in some parts of the world the sea is gaining on the land, while in other places it is as surely retreating; for we cannot believe that in one part the sea-level is rising, while in another (not far off in some cases) it is sinking. No body of water could behave in this irregular fashion; and the sea could not possibly be rising and falling at the same time.

Hence we may take it for granted that any change that we may notice in the relative level of land and sea must be due to upward or downward movements in the land.

But to return to Celsius. Old men pointed out to him various points on the coast, over which during their childhood the sea was wont to flow, and besides, showed him the water-lines which the waves had once traced out farther inland. And besides this, the names of places which implied a position on the shore, former harbours or ports now abandoned and situated inland, the remains of boats found far from the sea, and lastly, the written records and popular songs, left no doubt that the sea had retreated; and it seemed both to themselves and to the astronomer that the waters were sinking. In the year 1730 Celsius, after comparing all the evidence he had collected, announced that the Baltic had sunk three feet, four inches, every hundred years. In the course of the following year, in company with Linnæus, the naturalist, he made a mark at the base of a rock in the island of Leoffgrund, not far from Jelfe, and thirteen years afterwards was able to prove, as he thought, that the waters were still subsiding at the same rate, or a little faster. In reality, he had proved, not that the sea was sinking, but that the land was rising.

Similar observations show that nearly the whole of Scandinavia is slowly rising out of the sea. At the northern end of the Gulf of Bothnia the land is emerging at the rate of five feet, three inches, in a century; but by the side of the Aland Isles it only rises three and one quarter feet in the same time. South of this archipelago it rises still more slowly; and farther down, the line of shore does not alter as compared with the level of the sea.

But it is a curious fact that the extreme southern end of this peninsula is subsiding, as proved by the forests that have been submerged. Several streets of some towns there have already disappeared, and the coast has lost on the average a belt of land thirty-two yards in breadth.

The upward movement of the Scandinavian peninsula must have been going on for a long time, if we assume that it was always at the same rate as at present; for we find beds of seashells of living species at heights of six or seven hundred feet above the level of the sea. Great dead branches of a certain pink coral, found in the sea at a depth of over one hundred and fifty to three hundred fathoms, are now seen in water only ten or fifteen fathoms deep. It must have been killed as it was brought up into the upper and warmer layers of water. This is striking testimony.

The pine woods too, which clothe the hills, are continually being upheaved towards the lower limit of snow, and are gradually withering away in the cooler atmosphere; and wide belts of forest are composed of nothing but dead trees, although some of them have stood for centuries.

Geologists have proved that the Baltic Sea formerly communicated by a wide channel with the North Sea, the deepest depressions of which are now occupied by lakes in the southern part of Sweden; for considerable heaps of oyster-shells are now found in several places on the heights commanding these great lakes. Then we have in Denmark the celebrated "kitchen-middens," heaps of rubbish also largely composed of oyster-shells which the inhabitants, in the "Stone Age," collected from the bottoms of the neighbouring bays. At the present day the waters of the Baltic, into which rivers bring large quantities of fresh water, do not contain enough salt for oysters to grow there; but the oyster-shells prove that the Baltic Sea and these inland lakes were once as salt as the North Sea is now. This can only be explained by supposing that the Baltic was not so shut in then as it is in these days. The bed of the old wide channel has risen, and what once was sea is now land.

Again, it is very probable that the great lakes and innumerable sheets of water which fill all the granite basins of Finland have taken the place of an arm of the sea which once united the waters of the Baltic to those of the great Polar Ocean. And so there must have been upheaval here as well.

The old sea-beaches, now above the level of the highest tides, that are found in many parts of the Scandinavian, Scottish, and other coasts, furnish plain evidence of upheaval.

At the present day, between the lines of high tide and low tide, the sea is constantly engaged in producing sand and shingle, spreading them out upon the beach, mingling them with the remains of shells and other marine animals, and sometimes piling them up, sometimes sweeping them away. In this way a beach often resembles a terrace. When the land is upheaved rapidly enough to carry up this line of beach-deposits before they are washed away by the waves, they form a flat terrace, or what is known as a "raised beach." The old high-water mark is then inland; its sea-worn caves become in time coated with ferns and mosses; the old beach forms an admirable platform on which meadows, fields, villages, and towns spring up; and the sea goes on forming a new beach below and beyond the margin of the old one.

The Scottish coast-line, on both sides, is fringed with raised beaches, sometimes four or five occurring above each other, at heights of from twenty-five to seventy-five feet above the present high-water mark. Each of these lines of terrace marks a former lower level at which the land stood with regard to the sea; and the spaces between them represent the amount of each successive rise of the land. Each terrace was formed during a pause, or interval, in the upward movement, during which the waves had time to make a terrace, whereas, while the land kept on rising, they had no time to do so. Thus we learn that the upheaval of the country was interrupted by considerable pauses.

Sometimes old ports and harbours furnish evidence of upheaval. Thus, the former Roman port of Alaterva (Cramond) in Scotland, the quays of which are still visible, is now situated at some distance from the sea, and the ground on which it stands has risen at least twenty-four feet. In other places the scattered débris shows that the coast has risen twenty-six feet. And by a remarkable coincidence, the ancient wall of Antoninus, which in the time of the Romans stretched from sea to sea, and served as a barrier against the Picts, comes to an end at a point twenty-six feet above the level of high tides. In the estuary of the Clyde there are deposits of mud, containing rude canoes and other relics of human workmanship, several feet above the present high-water mark.

Raised beaches are found on many parts of the coast of Great Britain. Excellent examples occur on the coasts of Devon and Cornwall. On the sides of the mountainous fiords of Norway similar terraces are found up to more than six hundred feet above the sea; and as some of these rise to a greater height at a distance of fifty miles inland, it seems that there was a greater upward movement towards the interior of Norway than on the coasts.

There is a celebrated raised beach on the side of a mountain in North Wales, known as Moel Tryfaen, where the writer gathered a number of marine shells at a height of 1,357 feet.

But Scandinavia and Great Britain are not the only parts of Europe where an upward movement has taken place, for the islands of Nova Zembla and Spitzbergen show evidence of the same kind; and the coast of Siberia, for six hundred miles to the east of the river Lena, has also been upraised. On the banks of the Dwina and the Vega, 250 miles to the south of the White Sea, Murchison found beds of sand and mud with shells similar to those which inhabit the neighbouring seas, so well preserved that they had not lost their colours.

Again, the ground of the Siberian toundras is to a large extent covered with a thin coating of sand and fine clay, exactly similar to that which is now deposited on the shores of the Frozen Ocean. In this clay, the remains of the mammoth, or woolly elephant, now extinct, are preserved in great numbers.

Parts of Northern Greenland have also risen; while at the southern end of this frozen land a downward movement is still taking place.

The best-known example of these slow movements within historic times is the so-called Temple of Serapis in the Bay of Baie, near Naples. The ruins of this building, which was probably a Roman bath, consist of a square floor paved with marble, showing that it possessed a magnificent central court. This court, when perfect, was covered with a roof supported by forty-six fine columns, some of marble, others of granite. There is still a hot spring behind, from which water was conducted through a marble channel. All the columns but three were nearly buried in the soil which covered the whole court, when the ruins were first discovered. Now, each of the three marble columns that are still standing shows clear evidence of having been depressed below the sea-level, for they all exhibit a circular row of little holes bored by a certain marine shell-fish, known as Lithodomus dactylus, at a height of twelve feet from the floor; each row is about eight feet broad. The shells may still be seen inside the little pear-shaped holes which the shell-fish bored for themselves; and the same shell-fish still live in the waters of the Mediterranean and bore holes in the limestone rocks.

It is therefore quite clear that these columns must have been under water to a depth of twenty feet or so, and also that they must have remained under water for some considerable time, during which the shell-fish made these borings. Then an upheaval took place whereby the whole building was elevated to its present level. But underneath the present floor, at a depth of five feet, were discovered the remains of an older floor. This probably belonged to an earlier building which had in like manner been depressed below sea-level. We thus learn that the land in this spot had been sinking for a long time, and that at some subsequent time it rose. The fallen columns suggest the idea that they were thrown down by earthquakes. At the present time the land here is again sinking at the rate of one inch in three or four years.

But the first example of upheaval within comparatively recent times, and one which is instructive as throwing some light on the subject of the present chapter,—namely, the upheaval of mountain-chains,—is to be found along the western mountainous coast of South America. Here we have the magnificent ranges of the Andes running along the whole length of this continent. The illustrious Charles Darwin, during his famous trip in the "Beagle," discovered numerous raised beaches along this coast, and at once perceived their importance to the geologist. The terraces are not quite horizontal, but rise towards the south. On the frontier of Bolivia, they are seen at heights of from sixty-five to eighty feet above sea-level; but nearer the higher mass of the Chilian Andes they are found at one thousand feet, and near Valparaiso, in Chili, at thirteen hundred feet above the sea. Darwin also discovered that some of the upheavals thus indicated took place during the human period; for he found in one of the terraces opposite Callao, in Peru, at a height of eighty feet, shells with bones of birds, ears of wheat, plaited reeds, and cotton thread, showing that men had lived on the terrace. These relics of human industry are exactly similar to those that are found in the huacas, or burial-places, of the ancient Peruvians. There can be no doubt that the island of San Lorenzo, and probably the whole of the coast in its neighbourhood, have risen eighty feet or more since the Red Man inhabited the country.

Callao probably forms the northern limit of the long strip of coast that has been upheaved, and the island of Chiloe the southern limit; but even thus the region of elevation has a length from north to south of about 2,480 miles.

We noticed in the case of Scandinavia that the upward movement is greater in the interior of the mountain-range than at or near the coast; and it is interesting to find that the same difference has been observed in the case of the Andes. The upheaving force, whatever its nature, acts with more energy under the Chilian Andes than under the rocks of the adjacent coast.

In New Zealand we have also evidences of upheaval; and if we trace out on the map a long line from the Friendly Isles and Fiji, through the Eastern Archipelago, and then on through the Philippine Islands, and finally to Japan and the Kurile Islands, we shall find scattered regions of elevation all along this great line, which is probably a mountain-chain, partly submerged, and along which numerous active volcanoes are situated.

Putting together all the evidence that has been gathered on this subject, of which only a very small part is here given, we are warranted in concluding that taking the world generally, regions where active volcanoes exist are generally regions where upheaval is taking place. There is also a very interesting connection between mountain-chains and lines of volcanic action. From this it seems to follow, if lines of volcanic action are also lines of upheaval, that mountain-chains are undergoing upheaval at the present time. This is a conclusion in favour of which a good deal may be said. It is certainly true in the cases of the Scandinavian range, and also of a very large part of the Andes, to which we have already referred. The Highlands of Scotland and Scandinavia form the northern end of an old line of volcanic action running down the Atlantic Ocean through the Azores, Madeira, Cape Verde Islands, Ascension, St. Helena, right down to Tristan d'Acunha.

In many other parts of the world we have evidences from submerged forests, the positions of certain landmarks with regard to the sea, and in some cases submerged towns, that movements of a downward nature are taking place.

It is important to distinguish from these evidences the changes that take place where the waves of the sea are rapidly washing away the coast-line. Putting aside these cases, however, it has been clearly proved that in many regions a slow sinking of the land is going on.

The eastern side of South America has not been so thoroughly observed as its western side; but there is still good reason to believe that a large part of this coast is sinking. So it appears that a see-saw movement is affecting South America, and that while one side is going up, the other is going down; and it is interesting to observe other examples of the same thing,— such as are afforded by Greenland and Norway.

THE SKAEGGDALFORS, NORWAY.

FROM A PHOTOGRAPH BY J. VALENTINE.

Again, while part of Labrador is rising, parts of the eastern coast of North America, as far down as Florida, are slowly sinking. Thus along the New England coast between New York and Maine, and again along the Gulf of St. Lawrence, we find numerous submerged forests with quantities of trees standing upright with their roots in old forest-beds, but with the tops of their stumps some feet below the level of high tide. In the case of New Jersey the subsidence is probably taking place at the rate of two feet in a hundred years.

Before passing on to consider upward movements of a more rapid nature, such as are frequently caused by earthquakes, we may pause for a few moments to consider certain very slight, but nevertheless very interesting little movements, such as slight pulsations and tremors, which have been observed to take place in the earth's crust (as it is called), and which of late years have been carefully studied.

Professor Milne, a great authority on earthquakes, has noticed slight swayings of the earth, which though occupying a short time—from a few seconds to a few hours—are still too slow to produce a shock of any kind. These he calls "earth pulsations." They have been observed by means of delicate spirit-levels, the bubbles of which move with very slight changes of level at either end of the instrument. At present only a few experiments of this kind have been made; but they tell us that the surface of the earth (which is apparently so firm and immovable) is subject to slight but frequent oscillations. Some think that they depend upon changes in the weight of the atmosphere. If this is so, the balance between the forces at work below the earth's surface and those that operate on its surface must be very easily disturbed. Still we cannot see that this is a serious objection; on the contrary, there is much reason to think that any slight extra weight on the surface, such as might be caused by an increase of the pressure of the atmosphere, and still more by the accumulation of vast sedimentary deposits on the floor of the ocean, may be quite sufficient to cause a movement to take place. Moreover, Mr. G. H. Darwin has shown that the earth's crust daily heaves up and down under the attraction of the moon in the same kind of way that the ocean does; so that we must give up all idea of the solid earth being fixed and immovable, and must look upon it as a flexible body, like a ball of india-rubber (see chap. ix., pp. 314-315).

Slight movements of rather a different kind have been noticed, to which the name of "earth-tremors" has been given. These are very slight jarrings or quiverings of the earth, too slight to be observed by our unaided senses, but rendered visible by means of very delicate pendulums and other contrivances. Now wherever such observations have been made it has been discovered that the earth is constantly quivering as if it were a lump of jelly. In Italy, where this subject has been very carefully studied, the tremors that are continually going on are found to vary considerably in strength; for instance, when the weather is very disturbed and unsettled, the movements of the pendulum are often much greater. Again, before an earthquake the instrument shows that the tremors are more frequent and violent.

Another way of observing these curious little movements is by burying microphones in the ground. The microphone is a little instrument invented of late years which is capable of enormously magnifying the very slightest sounds, such as our ears will not detect. By its means one can hear, as some one said, "the tramp of a fly's foot," if he will be so obliging as to walk over it. It has thus been proved in Italy that the earth sends forth a confused medley of sounds caused by little crackings and snappings in the rocks below our feet.

In this way it will be possible to predict a serious earthquake, because it will give warning some days before, by the increase of the little tremors and sounds; and it is to be hoped that by this simple means human lives may be saved.

Now, these disturbances are of precisely the same nature as earthquakes,—in fact, we may call them microscopic earthquakes. To the geologist they are of great interest, as they seem to afford some little insight into the difficult question of the upheaval of mountains, and to show us something of the constant working of those wonderful forces below the surface of the earth by means of which continents are raised up out of the sea, and mountain-chains are elevated thousands of feet. It is probable that both are due to the working of the same forces, and are accomplished by the same machinery.

We now pass on to consider those more violent movements of the solid land known as earthquakes. This kind of disturbance is such as might be produced by a sudden shock or blow given below the ground, from which waves travel in all directions. First comes a rumbling noise like the roar of distant artillery; then come the earthquake waves one after another, causing the ground to rise and fall as a ship does on the waves of the sea; the ground is frequently rent asunder, so that chasms are formed, into which in some cases men and animals have been hurled alive. In the case of a very violent earthquake the waves travel long distances. Thus the great earthquake by which Lisbon was destroyed in the year 1755 disturbed the waters of Loch Lomond in Scotland. In this fearful catastrophe sixty thousand human beings perished. If the disturbance takes place near the sea, great sea waves are formed, which cause fearful destruction to life and property. This happened in the case of the Lisbon earthquake; and in the year 1868, when Ecuador and Peru were visited by a fearful earthquake, a great sea wave swept over the port of Arica, and in a few minutes every vessel in the harbour was either driven ashore or wrecked, and a man-of-war was swept inland for a quarter of a mile.

Earthquakes bring about many changes on the surface of the earth. For example, on mountain-slopes forests are shattered, and large masses of soil and débris are shaken loose from the rock on which they rested, and hurled into the valleys; streams are thus choked up, and sometimes lakes formed, either by the damming up of a river or by the subsidence of the ground.

It is frequently found after an earthquake that the level of the ground has been permanently altered; and this effect of earthquakes is important in connection with the subject we are now considering,—namely, how mountains are upheaved. Sometimes, it is true, the movement is a downward one; but more generally it takes place in an upward direction. As an example of this, we may mention the Chilian earthquake of 1835, which was very violent, and destroyed several towns on that coast, from Copiapo to Chile. It was afterwards found that the land in the Bay of Conception had been raised four or five feet. At the island of Santa Maria, to the southwest of this bay, the land was raised eight feet, and in one part ten feet; for beds of dead mussels were seen at that height above high water, and a considerable rocky flat that formerly was covered by the sea now became dry land. It was also proved by means of soundings that the sea round the island was shallower by about nine feet.

Now the question arises, "How are earthquakes caused?" Various suggestions have been made; but it is pretty clear that all earthquakes are not produced in the same way. For instance, volcanic eruptions are frequently attended by earthquakes. Violent shocks of this nature generally precede and accompany a great eruption, as is frequently the case before an eruption of Mount Vesuvius.

Steam plays a very important part in all volcanic eruptions; and these earthquakes are probably caused by great quantities of pent-up steam at a high pressure struggling to escape. It is also possible that when molten rock is forcibly injected into the crevices and joints of overlying rocks earthquake shocks may be produced by the concussion. The old Roman poet and philosopher, Lucretius, endeavoured to solve this problem, and concluded that "the shakings of the surface of the globe are occasioned by the falling in of enormous caverns which time has succeeded in destroying." But though the explanation might possibly apply to a few cases of small earthquakes, it is not a satisfactory one, for it is not at all likely that many large cavities exist below the earth's surface, because the great weight of the overlying rock would inevitably crush them in.

We have already pointed out that earthquakes frequently happen in mountainous regions; and this fact alone suggests that perhaps the same causes which upheave mountains may have something to do with earthquakes. But there are other reasons for believing that the same force which causes earthquakes also upheaves mountain-chains. The reader will remember the case of the Chilian earthquake that raised part of the Andes a few feet in height.

Now, it is quite clear that the rocks of which mountains are composed have suffered a great deal of disturbance. We have only to look at the crumbled and contorted strata to see that they have been forced into all kinds of positions, sometimes standing bolt upright (see diagrams, chap. ix., p. 307). And as we cannot believe, for many reasons, that these movements were of a very sudden or violent kind, we must consider that they took place slowly on the whole; but besides being folded and twisted, the rocks of mountains frequently exhibit clear signs of having been split and cracked. The fractures are of all sizes, from an inch or more up to hundreds or even thousands of feet. They tell us plainly that the rocks were once slowly bent, and that after a certain amount of bending had taken place, the strain put upon them became greater than they could bear, and consequently they snapped and split along certain lines. This is just what might be expected. For instance, ice on a pond will bend a good deal, but only up to a certain amount; after that, it cracks in long lines with a remarkably sharp and smooth fracture. But suppose the pressure came from below instead of from above, as when a number of people are skating on a pond. Should we not see the ice forced up in some places, so that some sheets stood up above the others after sliding past their broken edges? This is just what the rocks in different places have frequently done. After a fracture has taken place the rock on one side has slid up over the other, and the two surfaces made by the fracture—like two long walls—are no longer seen at the same level. One has been pushed up, while the other has gone down (see diagram of the ranges of the Great Basin, chap. viii., p. 273).

Now, it is almost impossible to conceive of these tremendous fractures taking place in the rocks below our feet without causing sudden jars or shocks. Here, then, we seem to have a clue to the problem. Even if the movements took place only a few inches or a few feet at a time, that does not spoil our theory, but rather favours it; for in that case the upheaval of a mountain-chain will have taken a very long time (which is almost certain), and may have been accomplished bit by bit. Hundreds and thousands of earthquake shocks, some slight, and others severe, may have attended the upheaval of a mountain-range.

This explanation is accepted by many authorities. It does not exactly imply that mountains were upheaved by earthquakes; but it means that the same forces that elevate continents, heaving them up out of the sea into ridges and very low arches, have been at work to crumple and fold their rocks in some places into stupendous folds, such as we now find form part of the general structure of mountains; and that in so doing they caused fearful strains, too great for the rocks to bear, so that they split over and over again, and in so doing produced jars and shocks that must have been very similar to, if not identical with, earthquake shocks as we know them at the present day.

Such an explanation is in striking harmony with what we have already learned about the operations of Nature. It was from the long-continued operation of rain and rivers that the materials now forming mountains were transported to the seas in which they were slowly formed. It was also by the ordinary operations of frost, heat and cold, snow and ice, streams, rain, and rivers that the mountains received their present shapes (see chapters v. and vii.). And now we learn that the gigantic work of upheaval took place in a tolerably quiet and uniform manner,—with perhaps only an occasional catastrophe of a more violent kind, but still according to the same law of uniformity which is the very basis of modern geology, and by means of which so much can be explained.

We could give other proofs of the gradual elevation of mountains if they were wanted. But at least enough has been said to give the reader a glimpse into the methods employed by geologists in endeavouring to explain how mountains were upheaved; and to show that it is only by a careful study of all that is taking place now on the earth that we can ever hope to solve the difficult questions that present themselves to all who study those stony records on which the earth has written for our enlightenment the chapters of her ancient history.

In conclusion, it may be asked what is the nature of the force that accomplishes all this titanic work of upheaval. Although the question has been much discussed, and some very ingenious suggestions brought forward, we cannot say that any of them are entirely satisfactory. But we know that the earth is a cooling body which loses so much heat every year; and it may be that the shrinking that takes place as it cools, by leaving the crust of the earth in some places unsupported, causes it to settle down, to adapt itself to a smaller surface below, and in so doing it would inevitably throw itself into a series of folds, or wrinkles, like those on the skin of a dried apple. Many think that mountain-ranges may be explained in this way.

CHAPTER VII.
HOW THE MOUNTAINS WERE CARVED OUT.

And surely the mountain fadeth away,

And the rock is removed out of its place,

The waters wear away the stones:

The overflowings thereof wash away the dust of the earth.

Job xiv. 18.

The mighty fortresses of the earth, which seem so imperishable, so majestic in their strength, and have from time immemorial received their title of "the everlasting hills," are nevertheless undergoing constant change and decay. They cannot abide for ever. Those waste leagues around their feet are loaded with the wrecks of what once belonged to them; they are witnesses to the victory of the hostile forces that are for ever contending with them, and pledges of a final triumph. To those who will read their story, mountains stand like old dismantled castles, mere wrecks of ruined masonry, that have nearly crumbled away, telling us of a time when all their separate peaks and crags were one solid mass, perhaps an elevated smooth plateau untouched by the rude hand of time.

Let us now inquire how the work of destruction is accomplished. Referring back to our illustration of the cathedral, given in chap. v., pp. 143-147, the question we have now to consider is, how the mountains were carved out into all these wonderful features of crag and precipice, peak and pass, which are such a source of delight to all who care for scenery. This work we included in the one word "ornamentation." What, then, are the tools which Nature uses in this work of carving out the hills? What are her axes and hammers, her chisels and saws?

This question, like many others, must be answered by observing what takes place at the present day. It is scarcely necessary to say that mountains and mountain-ranges are not simply the result of upheaval, though they have been upheaved. If that were so, they would probably appear as long smooth, monotonous ridges, with no separate mountain masses, no peaks, no glens or valleys; in some cases they might appear as simply elevated and smooth plateaux. Such mountains, if we may so call them, would be almost as uninteresting as the roof of a gabled house down which the rain finds its way in one smooth continuous sheet.

Mountains, reaching as they do into the higher regions of the atmosphere, where the winds blow more fiercely than on the plains below, storms rage more violently, and the extremes of heat and cold are more severe,—in fact, where every process of change and decay seems quickened,—suffer continually at the hands of the elements.

"Death must be upon the hills, and the cruelty of the tempests smite them, and the thorn and the briar spring up upon them; but they so smite as to bring their rocks into the fairest forms, and so spring as to make the very desert blossom as the rose."[23]

Nature never leaves them alone, never gives them a brief armistice in the long war that she wages against them. She is a relentless enemy, ever on the move, and ever varying her methods of attack. Now she assails them openly with her storm-clouds, and pelts them furiously with driving rain; now we hear the thunder of her artillery, as she pierces their crests with strange electric darts of fire; now she secretly undermines their sides with her hidden sources of water, till whole villages are destroyed by some fearful fall of overhanging rocks (see chapter iii., pages 96-101). Her winds and gentle breezes are for ever at work on their surfaces, causing them to crumble into dust much in the same way as iron turns to rust.

Again, she heats them by day and then chills them suddenly at night, under the cold starry sky, so that they crack under the strain of expanding and contracting. Now she splits them with her ice-wedges; now she furrows their sides with the dashing torrents and running streams; and yet again she wears them gently down with her glaciers, and carries away their débris—the token of her triumph—on those icy streams, as conquering armies carry the spoils in procession.

This is, briefly, her mode of warfare; these are some of her tools, wind, rain, frost, snow, heat and cold, streams, rivers, and glaciers. Lightning does occasionally break off portions of a cliff or a mountain-peak; but compared to the others, this agent is not very important.

Let us first inquire into the effects produced by the atmosphere. The air around us is composed mainly of two well-known gases; namely, oxygen and nitrogen. There is also a small proportion (about one in ten thousand) of carbonic acid gas; a variable quantity of water-vapour, and in the neighbourhood of towns, traces of other noxious gases, such as sulphurous acid and chlorine.

Now, the nitrogen plays a very unimportant part, as it merely serves to dilute the powerful gas, oxygen, which has such important life-sustaining properties. We live by breathing oxygen; so do all animals; and the more pure air we can contrive to get into our lungs, the better. But undiluted oxygen would be too strong for us, and so its strength is diminished by being mixed with four parts of nitrogen; that is to say, the air only contains about one fifth by volume, or bulk, of oxygen and four fifths of nitrogen.

Now, oxygen, being always ready to combine chemically with some other element, is a great agent of change and decay. It attacks all the metals except gold and platinum. Iron, we all know, oxidises, or rusts, only too quickly; but copper, lead, silver, and other metals are more or less attacked by it. So it is with all the rocks exposed at or near the surface of the earth. Oxygen will, if it can, pick out something to combine with and so bring about chemical changes which lead to decay. But a much more powerful agent is the carbonic acid gas in the atmosphere; although there is so little of it, there is enough to play a very important part in causing rocks to crumble away, and in some cases to dissolve them entirely. The supply of this gas is continually being renewed, for all living animals breathe out carbonic acid, and plants give it out by night. Under the influence of sunlight plants give out oxygen, so that gas is supplied to the air by day.

Both oxygen and carbonic acid gas are dissolved by rain as it falls through the air; and so we cannot separate the effects of the dry air by itself from those of rain and mist, which are more important agents. The action of rain is partly mechanical, partly chemical, for it not only beats against them, but it dissolves out certain mineral substances that they contain.

All rocks are mixtures of two or more kinds of minerals, the particles of each being often invisible to the naked eye. Thus granites are essentially mixtures of felspar, quartz, and mica; ordinary volcanic rocks ("trap-rocks") of felspar and augite; sandstones consist mainly of particles of silica; limestones of carbonate of lime; shales and slates of silicate of alumina, the principal substance in clay. These grains are usually joined together by a cement of some mineral differing more or less from the other particles. Lime is found in many of the rocks as the cement that binds their particles together; while oxide of iron and silica serve this purpose in many other instances. Now, if the lime or iron or silica is dissolved by water, the rock must tend to crumble away. Any old building shows more or less manifold signs of such decay, and this process is called "weathering." All this applies merely to the surfaces of rocks; and if there were no other forces at work, their rate of decay would be very slow.

But there are other forces at work. In the first place, sudden changes of temperature have a destructive influence. If the sun shines brightly by day, the rocks—especially in higher mountain regions—are considerably expanded by the heat they receive; and if a hot day is followed by a clear sky at night, the free radiation of heat into space (see chap. ii., p. 39) causes them to become very cold, and in cooling down they contract. In this way an internal strain is set up which is often greater than they can bear, and so they split and crack. Thus small pieces of rock are detached from a mountain-side. An Alpine traveller told the writer that one night when sleeping on a mountain-side, he heard stones rattling down at frequent intervals. Livingstone records in his journal that when in the desert he frequently heard stones splitting at night with a report like that of a pistol. But sometimes the expansion by day is sufficient to cause fragments of rock to be broken off.

Frost, however, is responsible for a vast amount of destruction among rocks. When water freezes, it expands with tremendous force; and this is the reason why water-pipes so frequently burst during a frost, though we don't find it out until the thaw comes,—followed by long plumbers' bills. Rocks, being traversed in several directions by cracks, allow the water to get into them, and this in freezing acts like a very powerful wedge; and so the rocks on the higher parts of the mountains are continually being split up by Nature's ice-wedge.

The amount of rock broken up in this way every year is enormous. Stone walls and buildings often suffer greatly from this cause during a long frost, especially if the stone be of a more than usually porous kind, that can take up a good deal of rain water.

Where trees, shrubs, etc., grow on rocks, the roots find their way into its natural divisions, widened by the action of rain soaking down into them; and as they grow, they slowly widen them, and in time portions are actually detached in this manner. Moreover, the roots and rootlets guide the rain water down into the cracks, or joints, as they are called. Even the ivy that creeps over old ruined walls has a decidedly destructive effect.

At the base of every steep mountain may be seen heaps of loose angular stones; sometimes these are covered with soil, and form long slopes on which trees and shrubs grow. Every one of the numerous little gullies that furrow the mountain-sides has at its lower end a similar little heap of stones. Sometimes a valley among the mountains seems half choked with rocky fragments; and if these were all removed, the valley would be deeper than it is. In some hot countries, where the streams only flow in winter, this is especially the case; for example, every valley, or "wady," in the region of Mount Sinai and Mount Horeb is more or less choked up with boulders and stones of every size, because the stones come down faster than they can be carried away.

But the main work of carving out the hills and mountains of the world is done by streams, rivers, and glaciers; and so we now pass on to consider how they perform their tasks. Water by itself, even when flowing fast, would be powerless to carve gorges and valleys in the solid rock; but the stones which torrents and streams carry along give them a marvellous grinding power, for with such material a stream continually wears away its rocky bed. Moreover, the stones themselves are all the while being rubbed down by each other, until finally they are ground down to fine sand and mud, which help in the work of erosion.

Every mountain stream or torrent runs in a ravine or valley of some sort; and any traveller who will take the trouble to watch what goes on there may easily convince himself that the ravine, gorge, or valley has been carved out by the stream, aided by the atmospheric influences to which we have already alluded.

But perhaps some may be inclined to look upon the ravine as a chasm produced by some violent disturbance from below, whereby the rocks were rent asunder, and that the stream somehow found its way into the rent. A little inquiry will dispel this idea. In the first place, such catastrophes are quite unknown at the present day; and as we have more than once pointed out, the geologist's method is to apply a knowledge of processes now in operation to the phenomena of the rocks, in order to read their history. Secondly, no conclusion can be accepted which is not supported strongly by evidence.

If such a rending of the rocks had taken place, there would assuredly be some evidence of the fact. We should expect to find a great crack running all along the bed of the stream; but of this there is no sign. Go down in any weather when the stream is low, and look at the rocks over which it flows, and you will search in vain for such evidence. Instead of being broken, the rocks extend continually across. You would also expect to find the strata "dipping," or sloping away from the stream on each side, if they had been rent by such an upheaval; but here again we are met by a total want of evidence. Thirdly, a crack might be expected to run along more or less evenly in one direction. But look at the ravine, follow it up for some miles, and you will see that it winds along in a very devious course, not in a straight line.

For these reasons, then, we must conclude that the ravine or valley has been carved out by the stream; but perhaps the most convincing arguments are afforded by the furrows and miniature ravines so frequently met with on the sides of all mountains; and it is impossible to examine these without concluding that they have in every case been cut out of the solid rock by the little rapid torrents that run along them after heavy rain. If we are fortunate enough to see them on a thoroughly rainy day, we may derive much instruction from watching the little torrents at work as they run down the mountain-side, here and there dashing over the rocks in little cascades, and bringing down to the base of the hill much of the débris that forms higher up. In this way Nature gives us an "object lesson," and seems to say: "Watch me at work here, and learn from such little operations how I work on a larger scale, and carve out my ravines and big valleys. Only give me plenty of time, and I can accomplish much greater feats than this."

The question of time is no longer disputed; and all geologists are willing to grant almost unlimited time, at least periods of time that seem to us unlimited. Most streams have been flowing for thousands of years; and when once we grant that, we find no difficulty in believing that all valleys are the work of rain and rivers. Surely no one would argue that the furrows on a mountain-side are all rents which have been widened by the action of water; for if they were rents, each must have been caused by some disturbance of the rocks composing the mountain, and we should of course be able to see the cracks for ourselves, and to find that the rocks had in some way been disturbed and rent open.

Even the rain which falls on the road in a heavy shower teaches the same simple but important lesson, as it runs off into the gutters on each side; and we may often find the road furrowed by little miniature rivers, that carve out for themselves tiny valleys as they run off into the gutter, bringing with them much débris in the form of mud and sand.

Sometimes a stream encounters in its course a layer of rock that is harder than the rock underlying it. In this case the softer rock is worn away faster, and the hard layer forms a kind of ridge at a higher level; the result is a waterfall. Waterfalls are frequently found in mountain streams. In this case, it is easy to trace the ridge of harder rock running unbroken across the path of the stream, showing clearly that it has not been rent in any way. First it showed merely as a kind of step, but gradually the force of the falling water told with greater effect on the softer rock below, wearing it away more rapidly than that above, and so the depth of the waterfall went on increasing year by year; and at the same time the hard layer was slowly worn away until the stream sawed its way through.

Some river valleys are steep and narrow; others are broad, with gently sloping sides. A careful study of the different valleys in any large country such as Great Britain, shows that their forms vary according to the nature of the rocks through which rivers flow. Where hard rocks abound, the valleys are steep and narrow; where soft rocks occur, the valleys are broad and low. This is only what might be expected, for hard rocks are not easily worn away; a river must cut its way through them, leaving cliffs on either side that cannot be wasted away by rain. But in a district where clay or soft sandstone occurs, the rain, as it finds its way to the valley, will wash them away and give a smooth gentle slope to the sides of the valley.

It is very instructive to notice how the scenery of any district depends on the nature of its prevailing rocks. Hard rocks give bold scenery with steep hills and rocky defiles; while soft rocks make the landscape comparatively flat and tame, though often very beautiful in its way, especially where a rich soil abounds, so that we see pleasant woods, rich pasture-land, and heavy crops in the fields.

Compare, for instance, the scenery of Kent or Surrey with that of the Lake District or the west of Yorkshire. The difference is due chiefly to the fact that in Kent and Surrey we have rocks that succumb more easily to the action of rain and rivers, and consequently are worn away more rapidly than the harder rocks in the north country. Geologists have a word to express the effects of this wear and tear; namely, "denudation," which means a stripping off, or laying bare.

In Kent and Surrey the agents of denudation (rain and rivers, aided by the effects of the air, of heat and cold, and so on) wear away the whole surface of the county in a tolerably even and uniform manner, because there are no hard rocks for them to contend with. In this case rain washes away the sides of the valleys faster than the river can carve its bed, consequently the valleys are shallow compared to their width. And so the streams have broad valleys, while the hills are smooth and gently rounded. Chalk, clay, and soft sandstone abound there. The two latter rocks are washed away with comparative ease, and the chalk is dissolved; whereas in the Lake District we have very much harder and older rocks, that require to be split up and broken by the action of frost, while every stream carves out for itself a steep valley, and great masses of hard rock stand out as bold hills or mountains, that seem to defy all the agents of denudation. Here the opposite is the case, and the valleys are deepened faster than they are widened. But for all that, a vast amount of solid rock has been removed from the surface there, of which the mountains are, as it were, but fragments that have escaped the general destruction. Moreover, the rocks in this region have been greatly disturbed and crumpled since they were first formed, and thereby thrown into various shapes that give certain peculiar structures more or less capable of resisting denudation.

Very effective illustrations of the power of rain by itself are afforded by the "earth pillars" of the Tyrol, and "cañons" of Colorado. The material of which they consist is called conglomerate, because it is composed of stones and large blocks of rock with stiff earth or clay between. All the taller ones have a big stone on the top which protects the softer material below from being washed away by heavy rains; and it is easily perceived that each pillar owes its existence to the stone on the top, which prevents the soft materials below it from being washed away. When, after a time, the weathering of the soft strata diminishes the support of the capping boulders, these at last topple over, and the pillar, thus left unprotected, becomes an easy prey to the rain, and is rapidly washed away. Some of the pillars are over a hundred feet in height. But it is only in places where heavy rains fall that these interesting monuments of denudation are to be seen.

By way of contrast we may turn now to a district in which very little rain falls, but where the streams have a considerable slope, and so can wear away, or erode, their valleys much faster than rain and frost, etc., can bring down the rocks of which the sides are composed.

The river Colorado of the West, which runs from the Rocky Mountains to the Gulf of California, flows for nearly three hundred miles at the bottom of a profound chasm, or cañon, being hemmed in by vertical walls which in some places are more than a mile in depth. The tributary streams flowing into the river run through smaller ravines forming side cañons; and there is no doubt that these wonderful chasms have been, in the course of ages, slowly carved out by the river Colorado and its numerous tributary streams. Sometimes the walls of the cañon are not more than fifty yards apart, and in height they vary from three thousand to six thousand feet.

Far above the level of the highest floods patches of gravel are found here and there on the sides, which must have been left there by the river when it had not cut its way so far down. These cañons afford striking testimony to the erosive power of running water, of which they are the most wonderful illustration in the world.

But water, even when in the form of ice, has more or less power to wear away solid rock; and the glaciers that we see in Switzerland, Norway, and other countries must slightly deepen the rocky valleys down which they flow. Let us see how this can be accomplished.

The snow that falls in the High Alps, impelled by the weight of fresh layers of snow overlying it, and by the slope of the mountain-sides, gradually creeps down into the valleys. Owing to the pressure thus put upon it, and partly to the melting power of the sun's rays, it assumes the form of ice; and glaciers are composed of solid ice. The downward motion is so slow that a glacier appears quite stationary; and it is only by putting in stakes and watching them change their positions that it can be shown to be moving.

In all respects except speed, glaciers flow like rivers, for ice is a viscous body, behaving partly like a fluid and yet partly like a solid substance; but it will not endure a sharp bend without snapping. Hence, a glacier in traversing a valley frequently gets split. The cracks thus formed widen by degrees until they expand into chasms, or "crevasses." Like rivers, glaciers transport a large amount of rocky matter to lower levels, and at the same time wear away and deepen their rocky channels.

Let us see how they do this twofold work of transportation and erosion. In the first place, a large amount of débris falls onto the sides of a glacier from the peaks, precipices, and mountain-side along which it flows. Some stones, however, fall down crevasses, and so reach the bottom, where they become cemented in the ice. In this way they are slowly carried down over the rocky floor of the valley, until at last they reach the end of the glacier, where in the warmer air the ice melts just as fast as it creeps down; and there they will be left to form a heap of stones, sand, and mud.

Large blocks of stone, quite different from the rocks on which they lie, are very numerous, and are called "erratics," since they are evidently wanderers from a distance. Sometimes such blocks can be proved to have been brought many miles from their home among the higher peaks. The long lines of stones and mud seen on the sides of a glacier are called "moraines," and at the end of every glacier we find a big heap known as a "terminal moraine." But the stones of which they are composed are probably not to be entirely accounted for in this way. Can we not conceive that the weight and pressure of a descending glacier may be sufficient to break off many protruding portions of the rocky bed over which it flows, and then to drag them along with it? This seems reasonable. Let us therefore consider the materials of which moraines are composed to be derived partly from the rocks beneath and partly from those above the glacier. But whatever their origin, such materials must inevitably find their way to the end of the glacier and be added to the big heap there. The work of transportation is then taken up by the stream which always flows from the end of a glacier. Such streams are in summer-time laden with fine sediment, which gives them a milky and turbid appearance.

Thus a glacier wears away the rocks over which it flows; rock fragments become embedded in the ice, and these are the tools with which a glacier does its work. It must be granted that the downward movement of a great mass of ice is irresistible, and consequently that as the moving glacier slowly creeps along, it must inevitably cause the stones which it thus holds to grind over the surface of the rock. It is easy to imagine the effects of this grinding action. If sand-paper, rubbed for a minute or two over wood, wears down and smooths its surface, what must be the result of all these stones, together with sand and mud, grinding over the rocky bed?

The answer to this question is found in examining the rocks over which glaciers once flowed. Now, the Swiss glaciers once extended far beyond their present limits; and the rocks in the lower parts of their present valleys, now free from ice, show unmistakable signs of having been considerably worn down. The corners and angles of projecting pieces of rock have been worn away until the once rugged outline has become wavy and round, so much so as to produce more or less resemblance to the backs of sheep lying down. Hence the name roches moutonnées, by which rocks of this shape are known. They frequently retain on their surface peculiar markings, such as long scratches and grooves which must have been made as the old glacier, with its embedded angular fragments of rock, slowly ground over their surfaces. Such markings are called "striæ." But besides these glacial records graven on the rocks, we have other evidence, in the form of great moraines in some of the valleys of Switzerland, and especially at those places where side valleys open out into a main valley. Any one may learn by a little observation to recognise these peculiar heaps of stones, mud, and sand, deposited long ago by the old glaciers of Switzerland.

It will be perceived that the evidence for the erosive power of glaciers is of two kinds,—first, there is the testimony of the smoothed and striated rocks, which is very convincing; secondly, the equally strong proofs from the moraines, both great and small. These old rubbish heaps give us a very fair idea of the amount of wear and tear that goes on under a glacier, for there we see the rock fragments that tumbled down the mountain-side onto the surface of the glacier (together with those which the glacier tore off its rocky bed), all considerably smoothed, worn down, and striated. But a still better idea of the work done is afforded by the gravel, mud, and sand in which these stones are embedded. All this finer material must have been the result of wear and tear. This kind of action may well be compared to what takes place on a grindstone as one sharpens an axe on it. The water poured on the stone soon becomes muddy, owing to the presence of countless little grains of sand worn off the grindstone. But a good deal of the mud thus formed is carried away by the little stream that runs out from the end of every glacier; so that there is more formed than we see in the moraine.

THE MER DE GLACE AND MONT BUET. From a
Photograph by Mr. Donkin.

We have already alluded in former chapters to the "Ice Age" in Britain, when great glaciers covered all our high mountains, and descended far and wide over the plains. Now, the evidence for the former existence of these glaciers is of the same kind as that which we have just described. In Wales and Scotland we may soon learn to recognise the roches moutonnées, the old moraine heaps, and the erratic boulders brought down by these old glaciers. Besides these proofs, there is also the evidence of the arctic plants now flourishing in the highlands (see chapter iv., pages 123-124).

There can be no doubt, then, that glaciers have an erosive action, and therefore must be regarded as agents of denudation. But it is important to bear in mind that their powers in this direction are limited; for it is manifest that a mountain stream is a much more powerful agent, and will deepen its little valley much more rapidly, than a cumbrous, slow-moving glacier, advancing at the rate of a few inches a day. It has been found by careful measurements that the Mer de Glace of Chamouni moves during summer and autumn at the average daily rate of twenty to twenty-seven inches in the centre, and thirteen to nineteen and one half inches near the side, where friction somewhat impedes its course. This seems very slow compared to the rapid movement of a mountain stream; but then, a glacier partly makes up for this by its great weight.

In considering a glacier as an agent of erosion, we must not forget that probably a good deal of water circulates beneath glaciers. If this is so, the water must have a considerable share in producing the effects to which we have already alluded. It would be extremely rash to conclude, as some students of glaciers have done, that valleys can be carved out entirely by glaciers; and we must be content with believing that they have been somewhat deepened by ice-action, and their features more or less altered, but no more. The valleys of Switzerland, of Wales, and Scotland, were probably all in existence before the period of the "Ice Age," having been carved out by streams in the usual way; but the glaciers, as it were, put the final touches and smoothed their surfaces.

Having learned how the three agents of denudation—namely, rain, rivers, and glaciers—accomplish their work, let us now take a wider view of the subject and consider the results of their united efforts both in the present and in the past.

We have already alluded to the enormous amount of solid matter brought down to the sea every year by rivers (see chap. v., pp. 166-168), and we pointed out that all this represents so much débris swept off the land through which the rivers flow; also that it comes down in three ways, one part being suspended in the water as fine mud, another part being pushed along the river-bed as gravel, etc., while a third part is the carbonate of lime and other mineral matter in a dissolved state, and therefore invisible.

Now, it is quite plain that rain and rivers, in sweeping away so much solid matter from the surface of the land, must tend in the course of time to lower its general level; and it therefore seems to follow that after the lapse of ages any given continent or large island might be entirely washed away, or in other words, reduced to the level of the sea. This would certainly happen were it not that the lands of the world seem to be slowly rising, so that the denudation going on at the surface appears to be counterbalanced by continued upheaval.

But, supposing no upheaval took place, how long would it take for rain and rivers to wear away a whole continent? Let us see if there is any way of answering this difficult question, for if it can be even partially solved, it will help us to realise the enormous length of time that must have been required to bring about the results of denudation that we see all around us.

Although the calculations that have been made on this subject are very complicated, yet the principle on which they are based is quite simple. For an answer to our question we must go to the rivers again, and measure the work they do in transporting solid matter down to the sea. Let us take the Mississippi as a typical big river, for it has been more carefully studied than any other, and it drains a very extensive area, embracing many varieties of climate, rock, and soil. As the result of many observations carried on continuously at different parts of the river for months together, the engineers who conducted the investigation found that the annual discharge of water by this river is about nineteen thousand millions of cubic feet, and that on the average the amount of sediment it contains is about a $1/1500^{th}$ part by weight. But besides the matter in suspension, they observed that a large amount of sand, gravel, and stones is being constantly pushed along the bottom of the river. This they estimated at over seven hundred and fifty millions of cubic feet. They also calculated that the Mississippi brings down every year more than eight hundred thousand million pounds of mud. Putting the two together, they found (as before stated) that the amount of solid matter thus transported down to the Gulf of Mexico may be represented by a layer 268 feet high, covering a space of one square mile; that is, without allowing for what is brought down dissolved in the water, which may be neglected in order to prevent any exaggeration.

Now, it is quite clear that all this débris must have come from the immense area that is drained by the Mississippi. It could not have been supplied by any rivers except those that are its tributaries. And so if we can find out what is the extent of this area, it is not difficult to calculate how much its general surface must have been lowered, or in other words, how much must have been worn away from it in order to supply all the material. This area is reckoned at 1,147,000 square miles; and a very simple calculation tells us that the general surface would thus be lowered to the extent of $1/6000^{th}$ part of a foot. That of course means that one foot would be worn away in six thousand years. On high ground and among mountains the rate of denudation would of course be much greater; but we are now dealing with an average for the whole surface.

The next thing we require to finish this calculation is the average or mean height of the American continent. This was reckoned by the celebrated Humboldt at 748 feet. Now if we may assume that all this continent is being worn down at the same rate of one foot in six thousand years (which is a reasonable assumption), we find, by a simple process of multiplication, that it would require about four and a half millions of years for rain and rivers to wash it all away until its surface was all at the sea-level (with perhaps a few little islands projecting here and there as relics of its vast denudation). This is a very interesting result; and if the above measurements are reliable, they afford us some idea of the rate at which denudation takes place at the present time.

By a similar process it has been calculated the British Isles might be levelled in about five and a half millions of years. Geologists do not pretend to have solved this problem accurately; that is impossible with our present knowledge. But even as rough estimates these results are very valuable, especially when we come to study the structure of the land in different countries, and to find out therefrom, by actual measurement, how much solid rock has been removed. We will now give some examples of this; but perhaps a simple illustration will make our meaning clearer.

Suppose we picked up an old pair of boots, and found the soles worn away in the centre. It would be easy to find out how much had been worn away over the holes by simply measuring the thickness of leather at the sides, where we will suppose that they were protected by strong nails. Geologists apply a very similar kind of method in order to find out how much rock has been removed from a certain region of the earth. One of the simplest cases of this kind is that of the area known as the Weald of Kent, Surrey, and Sussex (see illustration, Fig. 1). A great deal of denudation has taken place here, because there is ample evidence to prove that the great "formation" known as the Chalk (now seen in the North and South Downs) once stretched right across; and below this came the lower greensand and Weald clay. They spread over this area in a low arch of which we now only see the ruins.

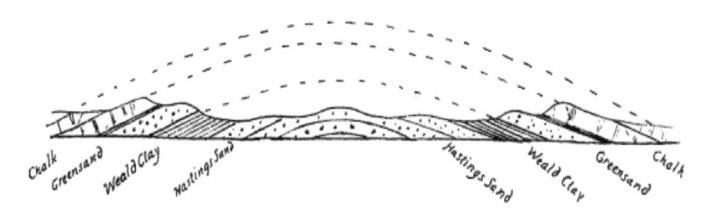

Fig. 1. SECTION ACROSS THE WEALD OF KENT AND SURREY.

Fig. 2. THE HIGHLANDS OF SCOTLAND ON A TRUE SCALE (after GEIKIE).

The dotted lines in the figure show us their former extent; but the vertical height is exaggerated, for otherwise the hills would scarcely be seen.

These lines simply follow out the curves taken by the strata at each end of the denuded arch, and therefore rightly indicate its former height. By making such a drawing on a true scale, geologists can easily measure the former height of the surface of this old arch, or "anticline," of chalk, greensand, and other strata, just as an architect might restore the outlines of an old traceried window from a few portions left at the sides.

This very useful and instructive method is much employed in drawing sections through mountain-chains, in order to gain some idea of the amount of denudation which they have suffered.

Let us see how much has been removed from the present surface of the Weald. First there is the chalk, which we may put down at six hundred feet at least; then there is the lower greensand, say, eight hundred feet; and below that, and forming the lowest ground in the Weald, is the Weald clay, which is one thousand feet thick, and being softer, was more rapidly borne away. Along the centre runs a ridge of Hastings sand, forming higher ground on account of its greater hardness, but this formation is not much denuded. However, adding together the thicknesses of the others, we arrive at the conclusion that about twenty-four hundred feet of chalk and other strata has been removed from the present surface of the Weald. And all this denudation has probably been effected by rain and rivers, for it is very doubtful whether the sea had any share in this work.

But in other parts of our own country we find proofs of denudation on a much grander scale than this; for example, in North Wales there are rocks now lying exposed at the surface which are of a very much greater antiquity than any that may be seen in the Wealden area, belonging to the very ancient periods known as the Cambrian and Silurian. These have evidently been exposed for a much longer time to the action of denuding forces; and the Welsh hills, as we now see them, are but fragments of what they once were. After carefully mapping out the rocks in the neighbourhood of Snowdon, noting their thickness, the directions in which they slope, or "dip," so that the structure of this region might be ascertained, as in the case of the Weald, it was found, on drawing sections of the rocks there, and putting in dotted lines to continue the curves and slopes of the strata as known at or near the surface, that from fifteen thousand to twenty thousand feet of solid rock must have been removed (see diagrams, chapter ix., p. 307). Applying the same method to the Lake District, it has been calculated that the amount of denudation which that beautiful country has suffered may be represented by twenty-six thousand feet. Turning to the other side of the Atlantic, we find the American geologists estimate that a thickness of five miles has been removed from a large part of the Appalachian chain of mountains (near their east coast), and that at least one mile has been eroded from the entire region between the Rocky and Wahsatch Mountains (see chapter ix.).

In conclusion, we must bear in mind that mountains, in spite of the enormous erosion they have suffered, are more capable of resisting the ever active agents of denudation than the softer rocks that form the plains and lowlands, and consequently stand out in bold relief from other features of the earth's surface. This truth has been beautifully expressed in the following passage:—

" ... In order to bring the world into the form which it now bears, it was not mere sculpture that was needed; the mountains could not stand for a day unless they were formed of materials altogether different from those which constitute the lower hills and the surfaces of the valleys. A harder substance had to be prepared for every mountain-chain, yet not so hard but that it might be capable of crumbling down into earth, fit to nourish the Alpine forest and the Alpine flowers; not so hard but that in the midst of the utmost majesty of its enthroned strength there should be seen on it the seal of death, and the writing of the same sentence that had gone forth against the human frame, 'Dust thou art and unto dust thou shalt return.' And with this perishable substance the most majestic forms were to be framed that were consistent with the safety of man, and the peak was to be lifted and the cliff rent as high and as steeply as was possible, in order yet to permit the shepherd to feed his flocks upon the slope, and the cottage to nestle beneath their shadow."[24]

CHAPTER VIII.
VOLCANIC MOUNTAINS.

'Tis said Enceladus' huge frame,

Heart-stricken by the avenging flame,

Is prisoned here, and underneath

Gasps through each vent his sulphurous breath;

And still as his tired side shifts round,

Trinacia echoes to the sound

Through all its length, while clouds of smoke

The living soul of ether choke.

VIRGIL: Æneid iii.

In some parts of the world we meet with mountains of a very different kind from any we have yet considered,—mountains that are known at times to send forth fiery streams of glowing lava, and to emit with terrific force great clouds of steam. Such mountains have long been known, in popular but unscientific language, as "burning mountains,"[25]—a term which is unfortunate, because they do not burn in the proper sense of the word, like candles or gas-jets. They are better known as volcanoes. There are about three hundred and fifty known active volcanoes; and if we include all mountains that once were in that state, the number is about one thousand.

Such mountains are connected in a curious way with those upheaved ridges of the world known as mountain-chains (see chap. vi., p. 191). And not only are many mountains more or less penetrated and intersected by rocks of an igneous origin (see chap. v., p. 155), but some have been largely formed by the action of old volcanoes. In fact, there are hills in Great Britain and parts of Europe, in America, and other countries, that once were actual volcanoes (see page 277).

We must briefly consider these strange mountains so different from others, and see what we can find out about them. Let us first inquire how a volcano is made, then consider what a volcano does; that is, we must view it as a geological agent that has a certain definite part to play in the economy of the world. And lastly, we may glance at some of the old volcanoes, and see what they were doing in those long ages of the world during which the great series of the stratified rocks were formed,—which rocks are, as it were, the book in which the earth has written her autobiography.

In old days volcanoes were regarded with superstitious awe; and any investigation of their actions would have been considered rash and impious in the highest degree. Mount Etna, as Virgil tells us, was supposed to mark the spot where the angry gods had buried Enceladus, one of the rebellious giants. Volcano, a certain "burning mountain" in the Lipa Islands, was likewise called the forge, or workshop, of Vulcan (or Volcan), the god of fire. And so it comes about that all "burning mountains" take their name from this one Mediterranean island, and at the same time tell us of the mythological origin of the word. It has been said that words are "fossil thoughts;" and we have here an old and very much fossilised thought,—a kind of thought long since extinct among civilised peoples, and one which is never likely to come to life again.

A volcanic mountain consists of alternating sheets of lava and volcanic ashes, mantling over each other in an irregular way, and all sloping away from the centre. In the centre is a pit or chimney, widening out towards the top so as to resemble a funnel or cup; hence the name "crater," which means a cup. In the centre of this crater a very small cone ("minor cone") is frequently found; and it is interesting to find that many of the moon's volcanic craters possess these "minor cones." A number of cracks or fissures intersect the volcano. These frequently spread out from the centre of the mountain in all directions, like the spokes of a wheel. They generally get filled with lava that wells up from below, thus forming "dykes," which may be regarded as so many sheets of igneous rock, such as basalt, that have forced their way while still liquid in among the layers of lava and ashes. The word "ash" is used by geologists in a special sense; and volcanic ash is not, as might be supposed, a deposit of cinders, but mostly of dust of various degrees of fineness, and sometimes it is very fine indeed. Pieces of pumice-stone may be embedded in a layer of volcanic ash, and sometimes great blocks of stone that have been shot out of the volcano as from a big gun, but these only form a small part of the layer. Dykes strengthen the mountain, and tend to hold it together when violently shaken during an eruption.

The shape and steepness of a volcano depend on the nature of the materials ejected. The finer the volcanic ash, the steeper and more conical is the mountain. The building up of a volcano may be fairly illustrated by the little cone of sand formed in an hourglass as the sand-grains fall. These settle down at a certain slope, or angle, at which they can remain, instead of falling down to the bottom, as they do directly this slope is exceeded. Some volcanoes are built up almost entirely of volcanic ash and its embedded blocks. Vesuvius, Teneriffe, Jorullo, in Mexico, and Cotopaxi, in the Andes, are examples of steep volcanic cones built up in this way. Others, less steep and more irregular in shape, are chiefly formed of successive lava-flows. Little minor cones are frequently formed on the side of a volcano; and these during an eruption give rise to small outbursts of their own. They are easily accounted for by the dykes which are mentioned just now; for when molten rock forces its way through fissures, it sometimes finds an outlet at the surface, and being full of steam, as soda-water is full of gas, it gives rise to an eruption. The great opening in the centre of a volcano, with its molten lava, is like a very big dyke that has reached the surface and so succeeded in producing an eruption.

The opening of a soda-water bottle not infrequently illustrates a volcanic eruption; for when the pent-up carbonic acid cannot escape fast enough, it forces out some of the water, even when the bottle is held upright.

Every volcano has been built up on a platform of ordinary stratified rocks; and at some period after these had been laid down in water and raised up into dry land, molten rock found its way through them, and so the volcano was built up by successive eruptions during many years. It is probable that earthquake shocks, preceding the first eruption, cracked up these strata, and so made a way for the lava to come up.

The main point we wish to emphasize is that volcanoes are never formed by upheaval. In this way they differ from all other mountains. They have not been made by the heaving up of strata, but have been gradually piled up, something like rubbish heaps that accumulate in the Thames barges as the dustmen empty their carts into them, only in the case of volcanoes the "rubbish" comes from below. It is not necessary to suppose that the reservoir down below, from which the molten rock is supplied, exists at any very great depth below the original land surface on which the volcano grows up.

The old "upheaval theory" of volcanoes, once advocated by certain authorities, instead of being based on actual evidence or on reasoning from facts, was a mere guess. Moreover, if the explanation we have given should not be sufficiently convincing, there is good proof furnished by the case of a small volcano near Vesuvius, the building of which was actually witnessed. It is called Monte Nuovo, or the New Mountain. It is a little cone 430 feet high, on the bank of Lake Averno, with a crater more than a mile and a half wide at the base. It was almost entirely formed during a single night in the year 1538, A. D. We have two accounts of the eruption to which it owes its existence; and each writer says distinctly that the mountain was formed by the falling of stones and ashes.

One witness says,—

"Stones and ashes were thrown up with a noise like the discharge of great artillery, in quantities which seemed as if they would cover the whole earth; and in four days their fall had formed a mountain in the valley between Monte Barbaro and Lake Averno, of not less than three miles in circumference, and almost as high as Monte Barbaro itself,—a thing incredible to those who have not seen it, that in so short a time so considerable a mountain should have been formed."

Another says,—

"Some of the stones were larger than an ox. The mud (ashes mixed with water) was at first very liquid, then less so, and in such quantities that with the help of the afore-mentioned stones a montain was raised one thousand paces in height."

(The writer's astonishment led him greatly to exaggerate the height.)

These accounts are important as showing how in a much longer time a big volcano may be built up. From such small operations we learn how Nature works on a large scale. The great volcano in Mexico known as Jorullo was probably built up in a very similar way. There is a tradition among the natives that it was made in two or three days; but we can hardly believe that. Volcanoes, as they get older, tend to grow taller and bigger; but every now and then a large portion may be blown away by some great eruption, and they have, as it were, to begin again.

THE ERUPTION OF VESUVIUS IN 1872. FROM AN INSTANTANEOUS PHOTOGRAPH.

Let us now consider volcanoes as geological agents, and see what they do. A volcanic eruption may be described in a general way as follows: Its advent is heralded by earthquakes affecting the mountain and the whole country round; loud underground explosions are heard, resembling the fire of distant artillery. The vibrations are chiefly transmitted through the ground; the mountain seems convulsed by internal throes, due, no doubt, to the efforts of the imprisoned steam and liquid rock to find an opening. These signs are accompanied by the drying up of wells and disappearance of springs, since the water finds its way down new cracks in the rocks, caused by the frequent shocks and quiverings. When at last an opening has been made, the eruption begins,—generally with one tremendous burst that shakes the whole mountain down to its foundations. After this, frequent explosions follow with great rapidity and increasing violence, generally from the crater. These are indicated by the globular masses of steam which are to be seen rising up in a tall column like that which issues from the funnel of a locomotive. But sometimes the whole mountain seems to be more or less engaged in giving out steam, and thus to be partly enveloped in it. This is illustrated by our engraving from an instantaneous photograph of Vesuvius in eruption in the year 1872. The steam and other gases, in their violent ascent, hurl up into the air a great deal of solid rock from the sides of the central opening, after first blowing out the stones which previously stopped up the orifice.

Blocks of stone falling down meet with others coming up; and so a tremendous pounding action takes place, the result of which is that great quantities of volcanic dust and ashes are produced, generally of extreme fineness. Winds and ocean currents transport these light materials for long distances. The observations made during the famous and fruitful voyage of H. M. S. "Challenger" showed that fine volcanic dust is carried by wind and marine currents to almost all parts of the oceans. The darkness so frequently mentioned in accounts of eruptions—sometimes at a very great distance from the volcano—is entirely caused by clouds of volcanic dust hiding the light of the sun. Perhaps the best example of this is the case of the eruption of Krakatoa (in the Strait of Sunda, between Sumatra and Java) in 1883. Its explosions were heard in all directions for two thousand miles, and a perceptible layer of volcanic dust fell at all places within one thousand miles; while the finest dust and vapour, shot up fifteen or twenty miles high, were spread all over the globe, causing, while still suspended in the atmosphere, the peculiar red sunsets noticed in all parts of the world for some months after the eruption.

Again, those very curious deposits of "red clay" found in the very deepest parts of the Pacific and Atlantic oceans (at depths of about four thousand fathoms, or twenty-four thousand feet) have been shown to be chiefly composed of volcanic dust, their red colour being due to oxidised iron.

But there is another way in which a good deal of fine volcanic dust is made; and it is this: the lava is so full of steam intimately mixed up with it that the steam, in its violent effort to escape, often blows the lava into mere dust.

Another interesting phenomenon may be thus described: Portions of liquid, or half liquid, lava are caught up by the steam and hurled into the air. These assume a more or less round form, and are known as "bombs." At a distance they give rise to the appearance of flames. And here we may remark that the flaring, coloured pictures of Etna or Vesuvius in eruption, which frequently may be seen, are by no means correct. The huge flames shooting up into the air are quite imaginary, but are probably suggested by the glare and bright reflection from glowing molten lava down in the crater.

So great is the force of the pent-up steam trying to escape that it frequently blows a large part of the volcano bodily away; and in some cases a whole mountain has been blown to pieces.

Finally, torrents of rain follow and accompany an eruption,—a result which clearly follows from the condensation of large volumes of steam expanding and rising up into the higher and cooler layers of the atmosphere. Vast quantities of volcanic ash are caught up by the rain, and in this way very large quantities of mud are washed down the sides of the mountain.

Sometimes the mud-flows are on a large scale, and descending with great force, bury a whole town. It was mostly in this way that the ancient cities of Herculaneum and Pompeii were buried by the great eruption of Vesuvius in the year 79 A. D., in which the elder Pliny lost his life. The discoveries made during excavations at Pompeii are of very great interest as illustrating old Roman life. The Italians give the name lava d'acqua, or water-lava, to flows of this kind, and they are greatly dreaded on account of their great rapidity. An ordinary lava-stream creeps slowly along, so that people have time to get out of the way; but in the case of mud-flows there is often no time to escape. No lava-stream has ever reached Pompeii since it was first built, although the foundations of the town stand upon an old lava-flood. Herculaneum is nearer to Vesuvius, and has at times been visited by lava-streams. Mud-lavas, ashes, and lava-streams have accumulated over this city to a depth of over seventy feet.

Lava-streams vary greatly in size; in some cases the lava, escaping from craters, comes to rest before reaching the base of the slopes of the volcano; in other cases a lava-flow not only reaches the plains below, but extends for many miles over the surrounding country. Hence lava-streams are important geological agents. Let us look at some famous instances. The most stupendous flow on record was that which took place from Skaptar Jökull in Iceland, in the year 1783. In this case a number of streams issued from the volcano, flooding the country far and wide, filling up river gorges which were in some cases six hundred feet deep and two hundred and fifty feet broad, and advancing into the alluvial plains in lakes of molten rock twelve to fifteen miles wide and one hundred feet deep. Two currents of lava which flowed in nearly opposite directions spread out with varying thickness according to the nature of the ground for forty and fifty miles respectively. Had this great eruption taken place in the south of England, all the country from the neighbourhood of London to that of Gloucester might have been covered by a flood of basalt of considerable thickness.

Sometimes, when the lava can only escape at a point low down on the mountain, a fountain of molten rock will spout high into the air. This has happened on Vesuvius and Etna. But in an eruption of Mauna Loa, in the Sandwich Islands, an unbroken fountain of lava, from two hundred to seven hundred feet high and one thousand feet broad, burst out at the base of the mountain; and again in April, 1888, the same thing happened on a still grander scale. In this case four fiery fountains continued to play for several weeks, sometimes throwing the glowing lava to a height of one thousand feet in the air. Surely there can be no more wonderful or awful sight than this in the world.

The volcanoes of Hawaii, the principal island in the Sandwich Islands, often send forth lava-streams covering an area of over one hundred square miles to a depth of one hundred feet or more; but they are discharged quite quietly, like water welling out of a spring. Repeated flows of this kind, however, have in the course of ages built up a great flat cone six miles high from the floor of the ocean, to form this lofty island, which is larger than Surrey; and it is calculated that the great volcanic mountain must contain enough material to cover the whole of the United States with a layer of rock fifty feet deep.

But it is not only on the surface of the land that volcanic eruptions take place; for in some cases the outbreak of a submarine eruption has been witnessed, and it is highly probable that in past geological ages many large eruptions of this nature have taken place. In the year 1783, an eruption took place about thirty miles off the west coast of Iceland. An island was built up from which glowing vapour and smoke came forth; but in a year or less the waves had washed everything away, leaving only a submerged reef. The island of Santorin, in the Greek Archipelago, is a partly submerged volcano.

But in some cases enormous outpourings of lava have taken place, not from volcanoes, but from openings of the ground here and there, and more usually from long fissures or cracks in the rocks lying at the surface. In many cases so much lava has quietly welled out in this way that the old features of the landscape have been completely buried up, and wide plains and plateaux formed over them. Sir A. Geikie says,—

"Some of the most remarkable examples of this type of volcanic structure occur in western North America. Among these that of the Snake River plain in Idaho may be briefly described.

"Surrounded on the north and east by lofty mountains, it stretches westward as an apparently boundless desert of sand and bare sheets of black basalt. A few streams descending into the plain from the hills are soon swallowed up and lost. The Snake River, however, flows across it, and has cut out of its lava bed a series of picturesque gorges and rapids.

"The extent of country which has been flooded with basalt in this and adjoining regions of Oregon and Washington has not yet been accurately surveyed, but has been estimated to cover a larger area than France and Great Britain combined. Looked at from any point on its surface, one of these lava plains appears as a vast level surface, like that of a lake bottom. This uniformity has been produced either by the lava rolling over a plain or lake bottom, or by the complete effacement of an original, undulating contour of the ground under hundreds of feet of lava in successive sheets. The lava, rolling up to the base of the mountains, has followed the sinuosities of their margin, as the waters of a lake follow its promontories and bays."

A few further examples of mud-lavas may be mentioned here. Cotopaxi, a great volcano in Ecuador, South America, with a height of 17,900 feet, reaches so high into the atmosphere that the higher parts are capped with snow. In June, 1877, a great eruption took place, during which the melting of snow and ice gave rise to torrents of mud and water, which rushed down the steep sides of the mountain, so that large blocks of ice were hurried along. The villages around to a distance of about seventy miles were buried under a deposit of mud, mixed with blocks of lava, ashes, pieces of wood, etc.

Sometimes a volcano discharges large quantities of mud directly from the crater. In this case the mud is not manufactured by the volcano itself, but finds its way through fissures and cracks from the bed of the neighbouring sea or rivers to the crater. Thus, in the year 1691, Imbaburu, one of the Andes of Quito, sent out floods of mud containing dead fish, the decay of which caused fever in the neighbourhood. In the same way the volcanoes of Java have often buried large tracts of fertile country under a covering of volcanic mud, thus causing great devastation.

Vast quantities of dust are produced, as already explained, by the pounding action that takes place during an eruption, as portions of rock in falling down meet others that are being hurled into the air. Striking instances of this have occurred not far from Great Britain. Thus in the year 1783, during an eruption of Skaptar Jökull, so great was the amount of dust thus created that the atmosphere in Iceland was loaded with it for several months. Carried by winds, it even reached the northern parts of Scotland, and in Caithness so much of it fell that the crops were destroyed. This is remarkable, considering that the distance was six hundred miles. Even in Holland and Norway there are traces of this great shower of dust from the Icelandic volcano.

During the fearful eruption of Tomboro, a volcano in the island of Sumbawa, in the Eastern Archipelago, in 1815, the abundance of ashes and dust ejected caused darkness at midday at Java, three hundred miles away, and even there the ground was covered to a depth of several inches. In Sumbawa itself the part of the island joining the mountain was entirely desolated, and all the houses destroyed, together with twelve thousand inhabitants. Trees and herbage were overwhelmed with pumice and volcanic dust. The floating pumice on the sea around formed a layer two feet, six inches thick, through which vessels forced their way with difficulty. From such facts as these it is clear that if in past ages volcanoes have been so powerfully active as they are now, we should expect to find lava-flows, dykes, and great deposits of volcanic ash deposited in water among the stratified rocks; and such is the case. Many large masses of rock familiar to the geologist, and often forming parts of existing mountains, are to be accounted for either as great lava-flows, or dykes that have forced their way in among the strata, or as extensive deposits of volcanic ash.

But perhaps the reader would like to know what the inside of a volcanic crater is like during an eruption. Let us, then, take a peep into that fearful crater of Kilauea, in the Sandwich Islands. For this purpose we cannot do better than follow Miss Bird's admirable description of her adventurous expedition to this crater:—

"The abyss, which really is at a height of four thousand feet, on the flank of Mauna Loa, has the appearance of a pit on a rolling plain. But such a pit! It is quite nine miles in circumference, and at its lowest area—which not long ago fell about three hundred feet, just as ice on a pond falls when the water below is withdrawn—covers six square miles. The depth of the crater varies from eight hundred to one thousand feet, according as the molten sea below is at flood or ebb. Signs of volcanic activity are present more or less throughout its whole depth, and for some distance round its margin, in the form of steam-cracks, jets of sulphurous vapour, blowing cones, accumulating deposits of acicular crystals of sulphur, etc., and the pit itself is constantly rent and shaken by earthquakes. Grand eruptions occurred with circumstances of indescribable terror and dignity; but Kilauea does not limit its activity to these outbursts, but has exhibited its marvellous phenomena through all known time in a lake or lakes on the southern part of the crater three miles from this side.

"This lake—the Hale-mau-mau, or 'House of Everlasting Fire,' of the Hawaiian mythology, the abode of the dreaded goddess Pele—is approachable with safety, except during an eruption. The spectacle, however, varies almost daily; and at times the level of the lava in the pit within a pit is so low, and the suffocating gases are evolved in such enormous quantities, that travellers are unable to see anything. There had been no news from it for a week; and as nothing was to be seen but a very faint bluish vapour hanging round its margin, the prospect was not encouraging.... After more than an hour of very difficult climbing, we reached the lowest level of the crater, pretty nearly a mile across, presenting from above the appearance of a sea at rest; but on crossing it, we found it to be an expanse of waves and convolutions of ashy-coloured lava, with huge cracks filled up with black iridescent rolls of lava only a few weeks old. Parts of it are very rough and ridgy, jammed together like field-ice, or compacted by rolls of lava, which may have swelled up from beneath; but the largest part of the area presents the appearance of huge coiled hawsers, the ropy formation of the lava rendering the illusion almost perfect. These are riven by deep cracks, which emit hot sulphurous vapours....

"As we ascended, the flow became hotter under our feet, as well as more porous and glistening. It was so hot that a shower of rain hissed as it fell upon it. The crust became increasingly insecure, and necessitated our walking in single file with the guide in front, to test the security of the footing. I fell through several times, and always into holes full of sulphurous steam so malignantly acid that my strong dogskin gloves were burned through as I raised myself on my hands.

"We had followed the lava-flow for thirty miles up to the crater's brink, and now we had toiled over recent lava for three hours, and by all calculation were close to the pit; yet there was no smoke or sign of fire, and I felt sure that the volcano had died out for once for our special disappointment....

"Suddenly, just above, and in front of us, gory drops were tossed in the air, and springing forwards we stood on the brink of Hale-mau-mau, which was about thirty-five feet below us. I think we all screamed. I know we all wept; but we were speechless, for a new glory and terror had been added to the earth. It is the most unutterable of wonderful things. The words of common speech are quite useless. It is unimaginable, indescribable; a sight to remember for ever; a sight which at once took possession of every faculty of sense and soul, removing one altogether out of the range of ordinary life. Here was the real 'bottomless pit,' 'the fire which is not quenched,' 'the place of Hell,' 'the lake which burneth with fire and brimstone,' 'the everlasting burnings,' 'the fiery sea whose waves are never weary.'[26] There were groanings, rumblings, and detonations, rushings, hissings, splashings, and the crashing sound of breakers on the coast; but it was the surging of fiery waves upon a fiery shore. But what can I write? Such words as jets, fountains, waves, spray, convey some idea of order and regularity, but here there was none. The inner lake, while we stood there, formed a sort of crater within itself; the whole lava sea rose about three feet; a blowing cone about eight feet high was formed; it was never the same two minutes together. And what we saw had no existence a month ago, and probably will be changed in every essential feature a month hence.... The prominent object was fire in motion; but the surface of the double lake was continually skimming over for a second or two with a cooled crust of a lustrous grey-white, like frosted silver, broken by jagged cracks of a bright rose-colour. The movement was nearly always from the sides to the centre; but the movement of the centre itself appeared independent, and always took a southerly direction. Before each outburst of agitation there was much hissing and throbbing, internal roaring, as of imprisoned gases. Now it seemed furious, demoniacal, as if no power on earth could bind it, then playful and sportive, then for a second languid, but only because it was accumulating fresh force.... Sometimes the whole lake ... took the form of mighty waves, and surging heavily against the partial barrier with a sound like the Pacific surf, lashed, tore, covered it, and threw itself over it in clots of living fire. It was all confusion, commotion, forces, terror, glory, majesty, mystery, and even beauty. And the colour, 'eye hath not seen' it! Molten metal hath not that crimson gleam, nor blood that living light."[27]

Continued observation of volcanoes, together with evidence derived from history, teaches that there are different stages of volcanic action. There are three pretty well-marked phases. First, the state of permanent eruption; this is not a dangerous state, because the steam keeps escaping all the time: the safety-valve is at work, and all goes smoothly. The second state is one of moderate activity, with more or less violent eruptions at brief intervals; this is rather dangerous, because at times the safety-valve does not work.

And thirdly, we have paroxysms of intense energy, alternating with long periods of repose sometimes lasting for centuries. These eruptions are extremely violent, and cause widespread destruction; the safety-valve has got jammed, and so the boiler bursts.

No volcano has been so carefully watched for a long time as Vesuvius. Its history illustrates the phases we have just mentioned. The first recorded eruption is that of A. D. 79, a very severe one of the violent type, by which

Herculaneum, Pompeii, and Stabiæ were buried. We have an interesting account by the younger Pliny. Before this great eruption took place, Vesuvius had been in a state of repose for eight hundred years, and if we may judge from the Greek and Roman writings, was not even suspected of being a volcano. Then followed an interval of rest until the reign of Severus, the second eruption taking place in the year 203. In the year 472, says Procopius, all Europe was covered more or less with volcanic ashes. Other eruptions followed at intervals, but there was complete repose for two centuries; that is, until the year 1306. In 1500 it was again active, then quiet again for one hundred and thirty years. In 1631 there took place another terrific outburst. After this many eruptions followed, and they have been frequent ever since. Vesuvius is therefore now in the second stage of moderate activity.

But geologists can take a wider view than this. They can sum up the history of a volcanic region of the earth; and the result is somewhat as follows: Volcanoes, like living creatures, go through different periods or phases, corresponding roughly to youth, middle age, old age, and finally decay. The invasion of any particular area of the earth's surface by the volcanic forces is heralded by underground shocks, or earthquakes. A little later on cracks are formed, as indicated by the rise of saline and hot springs, and the issuing of carbonic acid and other gases at the surface of the earth. As the underground activity becomes greater, the temperature of the springs and emitted gases increases; and at last a visible rent is formed, exposing highly heated and glowing rock below. From the fissure thus formed, the gas and vapours imprisoned in the molten rocks escape with such violence as to disperse the latter in the form of pumice and volcanic ash, or to cause them to pour out as lava-streams.

The action generally becomes confined to one or more points along the line of action (which is a line of fissures and cracks). In this way a chain of volcanoes is formed, which may become the seat of volcanic action for a long time.

When the volcanic energies have become somewhat exhausted, so that they cannot raise up the lava and expel it from the volcanic crater, nor rend the sides of the volcano and cause minor cones to grow up on their flanks, small cones may be formed at a lower level in the plains around the great central chain. These likewise are fed from fissures.

Later on, as the heated rock below cools down, the fissures are sealed up by lava that has become solid; and then the volcanoes fall, as it were, into the "sere and yellow leaf," and remain in a peaceful, quiet state befitting their old age.

After this they begin to suffer from long exposure to the atmospheric influences of decay, and rain and rivers wash them away more or less completely.

But still the presence of heated rocky matter at no great depth below is proved by the outbursts of gases and vapours, the forming of geysers and ordinary hot springs. Gradually, however, even these signs of heat below disappear; and the cycle of volcanic phases is at an end. Such a series of changes may require millions of years; but by the study of volcanoes in every stage of their growth and decline it is possible thus to sketch out an outline of their history.

It must be confessed that in the present state of scientific knowledge no full and complete explanation of volcanic action is possible. Geologists and others are as yet but feeling their way cautiously towards the light which, perhaps before long, will illumine the dark recesses of this mysterious subject. Many theories and ideas have been put forward, but in the opinion of the writer the most promising explanation is one that may be briefly expressed as follows:

There are below the crust of the earth large masses of highly heated rock that are kept solid by the enormous pressure of the overlying rocks, or otherwise they would melt,—for it is a known fact that pressure tends to prevent the melting of a solid body. But when earth-movements taking place within the earth's crust—such as the upheaving of mountain-chains—take off some of the weight, the balance between internal heat and the pressure from above is no longer maintained; and so these highly heated rocks run off into the liquid state, and finding their way to the surface through the fissures mentioned above, give rise to volcanic action. There is much to be said in favour of this view. It rightly connects volcanic action with movements of upheaval, with mountain-chains and lines of weakness in the earth's crust.

There is very good reason to believe that the earth was once in a highly heated state, and has been slowly cooling down for ages. The increase of temperature observed in penetrating mines tells us that it still retains below the surface some of its old heat. We need not therefore be surprised at the existence of heated masses of rock down below, or seek, as some have done, an entirely different source for the origin of volcanic heat than that which remains from the earth's once molten condition. It would take too long to state the reasons on which this idea of the former state of our planet is based, and moreover, it would bring us into the region of astronomy, with which we are not concerned at present.

In various parts of Great Britain and Ireland we meet with old volcanic rocks,—lavas, intrusive dykes, and sheets of basalt, etc., together with vast deposits of volcanic ash, which, sinking into the old neighbouring seas, became stratified, or arranged in layers like the ordinary sedimentary rocks. In some cases we see embedded in these layers the very "bombs" that were thrown out by the old volcanoes (see page 253). And besides these purely volcanic rocks, we often meet in these areas with great bosses of granite, which must have been in some way connected with the old volcanoes, and probably were in many cases the source from which much of the volcanic rock was derived. But more than this, in a few instances we have the site of the old volcano itself marked out by a kind of pipe, or "neck," now filled with some of its volcanic débris in the shape of coarse, rounded fragments (see page 277).

During a very ancient period, known to geologists as the Silurian Period, great lava-flows took place from volcanoes situated where North and South Wales and the Lake District now are; and by their eruptions a vast amount of volcanic ash was made, which fell into the sea and slowly sank to the bottom, so that the shell-fish living there were buried in the strata thus formed, and may now be seen in a fossilised condition.

Fig. 1. THE RANGES OF THE GREAT BASIN, WESTERN STATES OF NORTH AMERICA, SHOWING A SERIES OF GREAT FRACTURES AND TILTED MASSES OF ROCK.

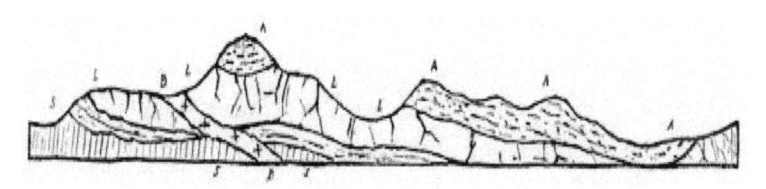

Fig. 2. SECTION THROUGH SNOWDON.

Thus Snowdon, Cader Idris, the Arans, Arenig Mountain, and others, are very largely made up of these ancient volcanic materials. The writer has picked up specimens of fossil shell-fish near the summit of Snowdon from a bed of fine volcanic ash that forms the summit. Fig. 2 represents a section through Snowdon, from which it will be seen that we have first a few sedimentary strata, S, then a great lava-flow, L; and that volcanic ashes accumulated on the top of this, of which A A are patches still left. B is an intrusive dyke of a basaltic rock that forced its way through afterwards. Again, in the Lake District there is a well-known volcanic series of stratified rocks of the same age, consisting mostly of lavas and ashes, the total thickness of which is about twelve thousand feet (known as the "Green Slates and Porphyries"), so that a large part of some of the mountains there have also been built up by volcanic action; but no traces of the old volcanoes remain.

Going farther north we find abundant proof that volcanic action on a prodigious scale took place in Scotland during the very ancient period of the Old Red Sandstone, with which the name of Hugh Miller will always be associated. In Central Scotland we see lava-flows and strata formed of volcanic ash, with a thickness of more than six thousand feet, fragments of which, having escaped the destructive agents of denudation, now form important chains of hills, such as the Pentland, Ochil, and Sidlaw ranges. Nor was the volcanic action confined to this region. In the district of the Cheviot Hills similar volcanic rocks are to be seen. But here again the old volcanoes have long since been swept away, leaving us only portions of their outpourings buried in the hills.

There can be no doubt that the present area of the Grampian Hills was once the site of a considerable number of volcanoes, only at a much higher level than their present surface, elevated though that is to the region of the clouds; but in this case subsequent denudation has been so enormous that the old mountain surface has been planed away until all we can now see is a series of separate patches of granite, that were once in a fused and highly heated state far below the surface, and formed part of the subterranean reservoirs from which the volcanoes derived their great supplies of lava and steam. It is indeed difficult to imagine the enormous amount of denudation which has taken place in the Highlands of Scotland, and to realise that the magnificent range of the Cairngorms, for instance, has been for ages worn down until now they are but a remnant of what they once were.

In this region we see the once boiling and seething masses of rock which fed the old volcanoes, now no longer endowed with life-like power by the force of steam, but lying in deathlike cold and stiffness, with their beautiful crystals of mica and felspar sparkling in the sun. The volcanic fires have died out; but the traces of their work are unmistakable, among which we must not forget to reckon the beautiful minerals made by the action of heated water upon the surrounding rocks.

The beautiful cairngorm stones are still sometimes found on the mountain from which they take their name, and in all volcanic regions minerals are plentiful.

The well-known hill called Arthur's Seat, close to Edinburgh, marks the site of an old volcano. The "neck," or central opening, may be seen at the top of the hill, but choked up with volcanic rocks and débris. The crater has long since disappeared, but Salisbury Craigs and St. Leonard's Craigs are formed of a great sheet of basalt that intruded itself among the stratified rocks that had been formed there, and so belong really to a great intrusive dyke. In the Castle Rock we see the same basalt again.

During a much later age, known as the Miocene Period (see chap. x., p. 324), enormous outpourings of lava took place in Western Europe, covering hundreds of square miles. Of these the most important is that which occupies a large part of the northeast of Ireland, and extends in patches through the Inner Hebrides and the Faröe Islands into Iceland. These eruptive rocks, unlike those above referred to, must have poured out at the surface, and have taken the form of successive sheets, such as we now see in the terraced plateaux of Skye, Eigg, Canna, Muck, Mull, and Morven. These, then, are patches of what once formed a great plain of basalt. During later times this volcanic platform has been so greatly cut up by the agents of denudation that it has been reduced to mere scattered fragments; thousands of feet of basalt have been worn away from it; deep and wide valleys have been carved out of it; and in many cases it has been almost entirely stripped off from the wide areas it once covered. Where, as in the Isle of Eigg, the lava has been piled up in successive sheets, with some layers of volcanic ash between, the latter has been worn away rather faster than the hard layers of basalt, and each lava-flow is clearly marked by a terrace. These volcanic eruptions have thus had a great influence in moulding the scenery of this region. In Ireland the old basalts are well seen at the Giant's Causeway, and on the Scottish coast we see them again at the well-known Fingal's cave at Staffa. This island, like the others, is just a patch of the old lava-streams.

Its curious six-sided columns illustrate a fact with regard to the subsequent cooling of lava-flows. Some internal forces, analogous to that which regulates the shapes of crystals, have caused it to crack along three sets of lines, so placed with regard to each other as to produce six-sided columns.

In Ireland the basalts attain a thickness of nine hundred feet; in Mull they are about three thousand feet thick. It has been clearly proved that Mull is the site of one of the old volcanoes of this period, but very few others have as yet been detected. Perhaps the eruptions took place mainly from large fissures, instead of from volcanic cones, for it is known that the ground below the lava-sheets has been rent by earthquakes into innumerable fissures, into which the basalt was injected from below.

In this way a vast number of "dykes" were formed. These have been traced by hundreds eastwards from this region across Scotland, and even the north of England. In this case the molten rock was struggling to get through the overlying rocks and escape at the surface; but apparently it did not succeed in so doing, for we do not find lava-flows to the east and south. These basalt dykes are found as far south as Yorkshire, and can be traced over an area of one hundred thousand square miles.

It is thus evident that in the Miocene Period a great and extensive mass of molten basalt was underlying a large part of the British Isles, and probably the weight of the thick rocks overlying it was sufficient to prevent its escape to the surface. If it had succeeded in so escaping and overflowing, how different the scenery of much of Scotland and Northern England might have been!

COLUMNAR BASALT AT CLAMSHELL CAVE, STAFFA. FROM A PHOTOGRAPH BY J. VALENTINE.

CHAPTER IX.
MOUNTAIN ARCHITECTURE.

The splendour falls on castle walls

And snowy summits old in story;

The long light shakes across the lakes,

And the wild cataract leaps in glory.

Blow, bugle, blow, set the wild echoes flying;

Blow, bugle; answer, echoes, dying, dying, dying.

TENNYSON.

The dying splendours of the sun slowly sinking and entering the "gates of the West" may well serve as a fitting emblem of the mountains in their beautiful old age, awaiting in silent and calm dignity the time when they also must be brought low, and sink in the waters of the ocean, as the sun appears daily to do. Yes, they too have their day. They too had their rising, when mighty forces brought them up out of their watery bed. Many of them have passed their hey-day of youth, and their midday; while others, far advanced in old age, are nearing the end of their course.

But as the sun rises once more over eastern seas to begin another day, so will the substance of the mountains be again heaved up after a long, long rest under the sea, and here and there will rise up from the plains to form the lofty mountain-ranges of a distant future.

Everywhere we read the same story, the same circle of changes. The Alpine peak that proudly rears its head to the clouds must surely be brought low, and finally come back to the same ocean from which those clouds arose. It is in this way that the balance between land and water is preserved. In passing through such a great circle of changes, the mountains assume various forms and shapes which are determined by:—

1. 1. Their different ages and states of decay.

2. 2. The different kinds of rocks of which they are composed, and especially by their "joints," or natural divisions.

3. 3. The different positions into which these rocky layers have been squeezed, pushed, and crumpled by those stupendous forces of upheaval of which we spoke in chapter vi.

Let us therefore glance at some of these external forms, and then look at the internal structure of mountains.

In so doing we shall find that we have yet a good deal more to learn about mountains and how they were made; and also we shall then be in a better position to realise not only how very much denudation they have suffered, but also how greatly they have been disturbed since their rocks were first made.

Every one who knows mountains must have observed how some are smooth and rounded, others sharp and jagged, with peaks and pinnacles standing out clearly against the sky; some square and massive, with steep walls forming precipices; others again spread out widely at their base, but the sloping sides end in a sharp point at the top, giving to the mountain the appearance of a cone. Their diversities of shape are so endless that we cannot attempt to describe them all.

First, with regard to the general features of mountains. Looked at broadly, a mountain-range is not a mere line of hills or mountains rising straight up from a plain on each side, such as school-boys often draw in their maps; very far from it. Take the Rocky Mountains, for instance. "It has been truly said of the Rocky Mountains that the word 'range' does not express it at all. It is a whole country populous with mountains. It is as if an ocean of molten granite had been caught by instant petrifaction when its billows were rolling heaven high."[28]

It has often been observed by mountain climbers that when they get to the top of a high mountain, and take a bird's-eye view of the country, all the mountain-tops seem to reach to about the same height, so that a line joining them would be almost level. For this reason, perhaps, writers so often compare them to the waves of an ocean. This feature is very conspicuous in the case of the Scotch Highlands.

Sir A. Geikie has well described what he saw from the top of Ben Nevis:—

"Much has been said and written about the wild, tumbled sea of the Highland Hills. But as he sits on his high perch, does it not strike the observer that there is after all a wonderful orderliness, and even monotony, in the waves of that wide sea? And when he has followed their undulations from north to south, all round the horizon, does it not seem to him that these mountain-tops and ridges tend somehow to rise to a general level; that, in short, there is not only on the great scale a marked similarity of contour about them, but a still more definite uniformity of average height? To many who have contented themselves with the bottom of the glen, and have looked with awe at the array of peaks and crags overhead, this statement will doubtless appear incredible. But let any one get fairly up to the summits and look along them, and he will not fail to see that the statement is nevertheless true. From the top of Ben Nevis this feature is impressively seen. Along the sky-line, the wide sweep of summits undulates up to a common level, varied here by a cone and there by the line of some strath or glen, but yet wonderfully persistent round the whole panorama. If, as sometimes happens in these airy regions, a bank of cloud with a level under-surface should descend upon the mountains, it will be seen to touch summit after summit, the long line of the cloud defining, like a great parallel ruler, the long level line of the ridges below. I have seen this feature brought out with picturesque vividness over the mountains of Knoydart and Glen Garry. Wreaths of filmy mist had been hovering in the upper air during the forenoon. Towards evening, under the influence of a cool breeze from the north, they gathered together into one long band that stretched for several miles straight as the sky-line of the distant sea, touching merely the higher summits and giving a horizon by which the general uniformity of level among the hills could be signally tested. Once or twice in a season one may be fortunate enough to get on the mountains above such a stratum of mist, which then seems to fill up the irregularities of the general platform of hill-tops, and to stretch out as a white phantom sea, from which the highest eminences rise up as little islets into the clear air of the morning.... Still more striking is the example furnished by the great central mass of the Grampians, comprising the Cairngorm Mountains and the great corries and precipices round the head of the Dee. This tract of rugged ground, when looked at from a distance, is found to present the character of a high, undulating plateau."[29]

This long level line of the Highland mountain-tops may be seen very well from the lower country outside; for example, from the isles of Skye and Eigg, where one may see the panorama between the heights of Applecross and the Point of Ardnamurchan showing very clearly the traces of the old table-land.

How are we to explain this curious fact, so opposed to our first impressions of a mountain region? It is quite clear that the old plateau thus marked out cannot be caused by the arrangement or position of the rocks of which the Highlands are composed. If these rocks were found to be lying pretty evenly in flat layers, or strata, undisturbed by great earth-movements, we could readily understand that they would form a plateau. But the reverse is the case: the rocks are everywhere thrown into folds, and frequently greatly displaced by "faults;" yet these important geological features have little or no connection with the external aspect of the country. It is therefore useless to look to internal structure for an explanation. We must look outside, and consider what has been for ages and ages taking place here.

As already pointed out, an enormous amount of solid rock has been removed from this region—thousands and thousands of feet. It was long ago planed down by the action of water, so that a table-land once existed of which the tops of the present mountains are isolated fragments. No other conclusion is possible. To the geologist every hill and valley throughout the whole length and breadth of the Highlands bears striking testimony to this enormous erosion. The explanation we are seeking may therefore be summed up in one word, "denudation." The valleys that now intersect the table-land have been carved out of it. If we could in imagination put back again onto the present surface what has been removed, we should have a mental picture of the Highlands as a wide, undulating table-land; and this rolling plain would suggest the bottom of the sea. The long flat surfaces of the Highland ridges, cut across the edges of inclined or even upright strata, are the fragments of a former base-line of erosion; that is, they represent the general submarine level to which the Highlands were reduced after exposure to the action of "rain and rivers," and finally of the sea. As the sea gradually spread over it, it planed down everything that had not been previously worn away, and so reduced the whole surface to one general level like the sea-bed of the present day. But it is not necessary to suppose that the whole region was under water at the same time, and it is probable that there were separate inland seas or lakes. In these the rocks of the Old Red Sandstone were formed; and they in their turn have suffered so much denudation that only patches and long strips of them are left on the borders of the Highlands.

Before we speak of individual mountains and their shapes, it is important to bear in mind another fact about mountain-chains; namely, that they are very low in proportion to their breadth and length. The great heights reached by some mountains produce such a powerful impression on our senses that we hardly realise how very insignificant they really are. It is only by drawing them on a true scale that we can realise this. The surface of the earth is so vast that even the highest mountains are in proportion but as the little roughnesses on the skin of an orange. Fig. 2 (see chap, vii., p. 236) represents a section through the Highlands, drawn on the same scale for height as for length.

What has been said about the Highland plateau applies equally well to many other mountain-ranges. Mr. Ruskin observed something rather similar in the Alps. He says,—

"The longer I stayed in the Alps, and the more closely I examined them, the more I was struck by the one broad fact of there being a vast Alpine plateau, or mass of elevated land, upon which nearly all the highest peaks stood like children set upon a table, removed, in most cases, far back from the edge of the plateau, as if for fear of their falling; ... and for the most part the great peaks are not allowed to come to the edge of it, but remain like the keeps of castles, withdrawn, surrounded league beyond league by comparatively level fields of mountains, over which the lapping sheets of glaciers writhe and flow, foaming about the feet of the dark central crests like the surf of an enormous sea-breaker hurled over a rounded rock and islanding some fragment of it in the midst. And the result of this arrangement is a kind of division of the whole of Switzerland into an upper and a lower mountain world,—the lower world consisting of rich valleys, bordered by steep but easily accessible, wooded banks of mountain, more or less divided by ravines, through which glimpses are caught of the higher Alps; the upper world, reached after the first steep banks of three thousand or four thousand feet in height have been surmounted, consisting of comparatively level but most desolate tracts of moor and rock, half covered by glacier, and stretching to the feet of the true pinnacles of the chain."

He then points out the wisdom of this arrangement, and shows how it protects the inhabitants from falling blocks and avalanches; and moreover, the masses of snow, if cast down at once into the warmer air, would melt too fast and cause furious inundations.

All the various kinds of rocks are differently affected by the atmospheric influences of decay, and so present different external appearances and shapes, so that after a little experience the geologist can recognize the presence of certain rocks by the kind of scenery they produce; and this knowledge is often of great use in helping him to unravel the geological structure of a difficult region. Thus granite, crystalline schists, slates, sandstones, and limestones, all "weather" in their own ways, and moreover split up differently, because their joints and other natural lines of division run in different ways.

Thus granite is jointed very regularly, some of the joints running straight down and others running horizontally, so that the rain and atmosphere seize on these lines and widen them very considerably; and thus the granite is weathered out either in tall upright columns, like those seen at Land's End, or else into great square-shaped blocks with their corners rounded off, presenting the appearance of a number of knapsacks lying one over the other. In this way we can account for the well-known "Tors" of Devonshire, and the "Rocking Stones." Granite weathers rapidly along its joints, and its surfaces crumble away more rapidly than might be expected, considering how hard a rock it is; but the felspar which is its chief mineral constituent is readily decomposed by rain water, which acts chemically upon it. The deposits of China clay in Devonshire are the result of the decomposition and washing away of the granite of Dartmoor.

Granite mountains are generally rounded and "bossy," breaking now and then into cliffs, the faces of which are riven by huge joints, and present a very different appearance from those composed of crystalline schists with their sharp crests and peaks. Ben Nevis and the Cairngorms are partly composed of granite.

Gneiss is a rock composed of the same minerals as granite; namely, mica, quartz, and felspar. And yet mountains composed of this rock have quite a different aspect, and sometimes, as in the Alps, produce very sharp and jagged pinnacles. The reason of this is that gneiss splits in a different way from granite, because its minerals are arranged in layers, and so it is more like a crystalline schist.

Mica-schist is another rock very abundant in mountain regions. This rock is composed of quartz and mica arranged in wavy layers. The mica, which is very conspicuous, lies in thin plates, sometimes so dovetailed into each other as to form long continuous layers separating it from those of the quartz; and it readily splits along the layers of mica. This mineral is easily recognised by its bright, shiny surface. There are, however, two varieties,— one of a light colour and the other black.

Mica-schist and gneiss are often found in the same region, and are the materials of which most of the highest peaks in Europe are composed. We find them abounding in the district of Mont Blanc; and all the monarch's attendant aiguilles, with the splintered ridges enclosing the great snowfields in the heart of the chain, consist mostly of these two rocks. The Matterhorn, Weisshorn, Monte Viso, the Grand Paradis, the Aiguille Verte and Aiguille du Dru are examples of the wonderful forms produced by the breaking up and decay of these two rocks.

The different varieties of slate split in a very marked way. Slates are often associated with the schists, and exert their influence in modifying the scenery.

Limestone ranges, though less striking in the outlines of their crests than those composed of slates and crystalline schists, and not reaching to such heights, are nevertheless not at all inferior in the grandeur of their cliffs, which frequently extend for miles along the side of a valley in vast terraces, whose precipitous walls are often absolutely inaccessible. The beauty of limestone mountains is often enhanced by the rich pastures and forests which clothe their lower slopes. The dolomitic limestone of the Italian Tyrol, being gashed by enormous vertical joints and at the same time having been formed in rather thin layers which break up into small blocks, produces some very striking scenery. But wild as these mountainous ridges may be, their forms can never be confounded with those of the crystalline schists; for however sharp their pinnacles may appear at first sight, careful examination will always show that their outline is that of ruined masonry, suggesting crumbling battlements and tottering turrets, and not the curving, flame-like crests and splintered peaks of the crystalline schists.[30]

It has already been explained that all sedimentary rocks have been formed under water in layers or strata, and it must be obvious that the stratification of such rocks has an important influence on scenery; and very much depends on whether the strata have been left undisturbed, with perhaps just a slight slope, or whether they have been folded and crumpled; for the position of the strata, or "bedding," as it is called,—whether flat, inclined, vertical, or contorted,—largely determines the nature of the surface. Undoubtedly the most characteristic scenery formed by stratified rocks is to be seen in those places where the "bedding" is horizontal, or nearly so, and the strata are massive. A mountain constructed of such materials appears as a colossal pyramid, the level lines of stratification looking like great courses of masonry. The joints that cut across the strata allow it to be cleft into great blocks and deep chasms; so that, as in the case of the dolomitic limestone above mentioned, we find a resemblance to ruined buildings.

We cannot find a better example of this in our own country than the mountains of sandstone and conglomerate (of the Cambrian age) that here and there lie on the great platform of old gneiss in the west of Sutherland and Ross. Sir A. Geikie says,—

"The bleak, bare gneiss, with its monotonous undulations, tarns, and bogs, is surmounted by groups of cones, which for individuality of form and independence of position better deserve to be called mountains than most of the eminences to which that name is given in Scotland. These huge pyramids, rising to heights of between two thousand and four thousand feet, consist of dark red strata, so little inclined that their edges can be traced by the eye in long, level bars on the steeper hillsides and precipices, like lines of masonry. Here and there the hand of time has rent them into deep rifts, from which long 'screes' (slopes of loose stones) descend into the plains below, as stones are detached from the shivered walls of an ancient battlement. Down their sides, which have in places the steepness of a bastion, vegetation finds but scanty room along the projecting ledges of the sandstone beds, where the heath and grass and wildflowers cluster over the rock in straggling lines and tufts of green; and yet, though nearly as bare as the gneiss below them, these lofty mountains are far from presenting the same aspect of barrenness. The prevailing colour of their component strata gives them a warm red hue, which even at noon contrasts strongly with the grey of the platform of older rock.... These huge isolated cones are among the most striking memorials of denudation anywhere to be seen in the British Isles. Quinag, Canisp, Suilven, Coulmore, and the hills of Coygoch,

Dundonald, Loch Maree, and Torridon are merely detached patches of a formation not less than seven thousand or eight thousand feet thick, which once spread over the northwest of Scotland. The spaces between them were once occupied by the same dull red sandstone; the horizontal stratification of one hill, indeed, is plainly continuous with that of the others, though deep and wide valleys, or miles of low moorland, may now lie between. While the valleys have been worn down through the sandstone, these strange pyramidal mountains that form so singular a feature in the landscapes of the northwest highlands have been left standing, like lonely sea-stacks, as monuments of long ages of waste."[31]

Again, the vast table-lands of the Colorado region illustrate on a truly magnificent scale, to which there is no parallel in the Old World, the effects of atmospheric erosion on undisturbed and nearly level strata. Here we find valleys and river gorges deeper and longer than any others in the world; great winding lines of escarpment, like ranges of sea cliffs; terraced slopes rising at various levels; huge buttresses and solitary monuments, standing like islands out of the plains; and lastly, great mountain masses carved out into the most striking and picturesque shapes, yet with their lines of "bedding" clearly marked out.

On the other hand, where, as is almost always the case in mountain-ranges, the stratified rocks have been folded, crumpled, twisted, and fractured by great "faults," we find a very different result. In these cases the rocks have generally been very much altered by the action of heat. For here we find crystalline schists, gneiss, granite, and other rocks in the formation of which heat has played an important part; and very often the igneous rocks have forced their way through those of sedimentary origin and altered them into what are called metamorphic rocks (see chapter v., page [156](#)). Thus they have lost much of their original character and structure.

The repeated uplifts and subsidences of the earth's crust, by which the continents of the world have been raised up out of the sea to form dry land, have, broadly speaking, thrown the rocky strata into a series of wave-like undulations. In some extensive regions these undulations are so broad and low that the curvature is quite imperceptible, and the strata appear to lie in horizontal layers, or to slope very slightly in a certain direction. This is, in a general way, the position of the strata of which plains and plateaux are composed.

But in the longer and comparatively narrow mountain regions that traverse each of the great continents, forming, as it were, backbones to them, the undulations are very much more frequent, narrower, and higher. Sometimes the rocks have been thrown into huge open waves, or the folds are closely crowded together, so that the strata stand on their ends, or are even completely overturned, and thus their proper order of succession is reversed, and the older ones actually lie on the top of the newer ones.

As we approach a great mountain-chain we observe many minor ridges and smaller chains running roughly parallel with it, and, as it were, foreshadowing the great folds met with in the centre of the chain and among its highest peaks. These small folds become sharper and closer the nearer we get to the main chain, and evidently were formed by the same movements that uplifted the higher ranges beyond; but the force was not so great. Thus we find the great Alpine chain flanked to the north by the smaller ranges of the Jura Mountains; and on the south, side of the Himalayas we find similar smaller ranges of hills.

Ruskin thus describes his impression of the Jura ranges, which he very aptly compares with a swell on the sea far away from a storm, the storm being represented by the wild sea of Alpine mountains:—

"Among the hours of his life to which the writer looks back with peculiar gratitude, as having been marked with more than ordinary fulness of joy or clearness of teaching, is one passed, now some years ago, near time of sunset, among the masses of pine forest which skirt the course of the Ain, above the village of Champagnole, in the Jura. It is a spot which has all the solemnity, with none of the savageness, of the Alps; where there is a sense of a great power beginning to be manifested in the earth, and of a deep and majestic concord in the rise of the long low lines of piny hills,—the first utterance of those mighty mountain symphonies, soon to be more loudly lifted and wildly broken along the battlements of the Alps. But their strength is as yet restrained; and the far-reaching ridges of pastoral mountain succeed each other, like the long and sighing swell which moves over quiet waters from some far-off stormy sea.

"And there is a deep tenderness pervading that vast monotony. The destructive forces and the stern expression of the central ranges are alike withdrawn. No frost-ploughed, dust-encumbered paths of ancient glacier fret the soft Jura pastures; no splintered heaps of ruin break the fair ranks of her forests; no pale, defiled, or furious rivers rend their rude and changeful ways among her rocks. Patiently, eddy by eddy, the clear green streams wind along their well-known beds; and under the dark quietness of the undisturbed pines there spring up, year by year, such company of joyful flowers as I know not the like among all the blessings of the earth."

Long faults, or fractures, where the strata have been first bent and then broken, and afterwards have been forced up or have slid down hundreds or even thousands of feet, are very numerous in mountain-ranges; and by suddenly bringing quite a different set of rocks to the surface, these faults cause considerable difficulty to the geologist, as he goes over the ground and endeavours to trace the positions of the different rocks.

In these vast folds it sometimes happens that portions of older (and lower) strata are caught up and so embedded among those of newer rocks. It will therefore be readily perceived that to unravel the geological structure of a great mountain-chain is no easy task. We need not then be surprised if in some cases the arrangement of the rocks of mountains is not thoroughly understood. The wonder is, when we think of the numerous difficulties which the geologist encounters,—the arduous ascents, the precipices, glaciers, snowfields obscuring the rocks from his view, the overlying soil of the lower parts, and the steep crests and dangerous ridges that separate the snowfields,—that so much has already been discovered in this difficult branch of geology.

However, the general arrangement of the rocks of which many mountain-chains are composed has been satisfactorily made out in not a few cases. Let us look into some of these and see what has been discovered.

You will remember the structure of the Weald, described in chap. vii., pp. 235-238, and how we showed that a great low arch of chalk strata has been entirely removed over that area, so that at the present time only its ends are seen forming the escarpments of the North and South Downs. This area, then, is now a great open valley, or rather a gently undulating plain enclosed by low chalk hills. Now, an arch of this kind is called an "anticline," and it might have been expected that it would have remained more or less unbroken to the present day. Why, then, has it suffered destruction?

In the first place, chalk is a soft rock, and one that rain water can dissolve; but more than that, its arch-like structure was against it, and its chance of preservation was decidedly small. In architecture the arch is the most firm and stable structure that can be made; but not so with strata, and this is the reason. Such an arch was not made of separate blocks, closely fitting and firmly cemented together; on the contrary, the arch was stretched and heaved up from below. It therefore must have been more or less cracked up; for rocks are apt to split when bent, although when deeply buried under a great thickness of overlying rocks, they will bend very considerably without snapping. But this was not the case here. And so the forces of denudation set to work upon an already somewhat broken mass of rock. Try to picture to yourself this old low arch of chalk as it was when it first appeared as dry land. Probably some of it had already been planed away by the waves of the sea, and what was left was by no means well calculated to withstand the action of the agents of denudation. If you look back to the figure, you will see the dotted lines showing the former outline of this anticline, or arch, and you perceive at once that the strata must have been sloping outwards away from the middle. Now, this one fact greatly influenced its fate, for an anticline cannot be regarded as a strong or stable arrangement of strata. It is easy to see why; suppose a little portion were cut away on one side at its base by some stream. It is clear that a kind of overhanging cliff would be left, and blocks of chalk would sooner or later come rolling down into the valley of the little stream. When these had fallen, they would leave an inclined plane down which others would follow; and this would continue to take place until the top of the arch was reached. The same reasoning applies to the other side. It is very seldom that arches, or anticlines, can last for a long time. The outward slope of the strata and their broken condition are against them.

But when the rocks dip inwards, to form a kind of trough or basin, it is just the opposite. Such basins are known as "synclines;" and a structure of this kind can be shown to be much more stable and permanent than an anticline. The strata, instead of being stretched out and cracked open, have been squeezed together.

It is very important to bear this in mind, and to remember how differently anticlines and synclines are affected; for this simple rule is illustrated over and over again in mountain-ranges:—

Anticlines, being unstable, are worn away until they become valleys.

Synclines, being stable, are left and frequently form mountains.

Now look at the section through the Appalachian chain (see Fig. 1), and you will see that each hill is a syncline, and the valleys between them are anticlines. This happens so frequently that almost every range of mountains furnishes examples; but as every rule has its exceptions, so this one has, and we may find an example in the case of the Jura Mountains outside the Alps.

It will be seen from the section that the ridges are formed by anticlines, and the valleys by synclines. But on looking a little more closely, we see that the tops of the former have suffered a considerable amount of erosion (as indicated by the dotted lines). Now, the reason why they have not been completely worn down into valleys is that these rocks were once covered by others overlying them, so that this outer covering of rocks had first to be removed before they could be attacked by rain and rivers. These wave-like ridges of the Jura are being slowly worn down; and the time must come when they will be carved out into valleys, while the synclines between them will stand out as hills. It is simply a question of time. But many mountain-chains have a far more complicated structure than that of the Appalachians, and consist of violently crumpled and folded strata (see section of Mont Blanc, Fig. 3).

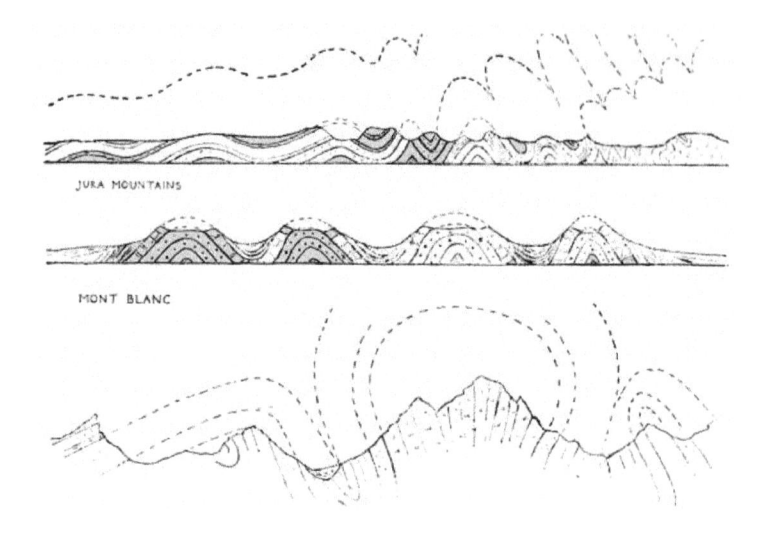

SECTIONS OF MOUNTAIN-RANGES, SHOWING THEIR STRUCTURE AND THE AMOUNT OF ROCK WORN AWAY.

It might naturally be asked how such sections are made, considering that we cannot cut through mountains in order to find out their structure; but Nature cuts them up for us, gashing their sides with ravines and valleys carved out by streams and rivers, and in steep cliffs and precipices we find great natural sections that serve our purpose almost equally well. Sometimes, however, we get considerable help from quarries and railway-cuttings.

Take, for example, one of the synclinal folds in the Appalachian chain. Its structure is ascertained somewhat as follows. Suppose you began to ascend the hill, armed with a good map, a pocket-compass, a clinometer,—a little instrument for measuring the angles at which strata dip or slope,—and with a bag on your back for specimens of rocks and fossils. At the base of the hill you might notice at starting a certain layer of rock—say a limestone—exposed by the side of the stream. It will be so many feet thick, and will contain such-and-such fossils, by means of which you can identify it; and it will dip into the interior of the hill at a certain angle, as measured by the clinometer. As you rise higher, this rock may be succeeded by sandstone of a certain thickness, and likewise dipping into the hill; and so with the other rocks that follow, until you reach the summit.

By the time you have reached the top of the hill, you know the nature of all the rocks up that side, and the way they dip; and all your observations are carefully recorded in a notebook. Then you begin to descend on the other side, and in so doing you find the same set of rocks coming out at the surface all in the same order; only this order is now reversed, because you are following them downwards instead of upwards. Of course they are hidden in many places by soil and loose stones; but that does not matter, because at other places they are exposed to view, especially along ravines, carved out of the mountain-side. Also rocks "weather" so differently that they can often be distinguished even at a distance.

In this kind of way you can find out the structure of a mountain, and draw a section of it when you get home, by following out and completing the curves of the strata as indicated at or near the surface; and you find they fit in nicely together.

Fig. 3 (see page 307) represents what is believed to be the general arrangement of the rocks of Mont Blanc. The section is greatly simplified, because many minor folds and all the faults, or dislocations, are omitted. Now, in this case we have an example of what is known as the "fan-structure." It will be seen at once that the folds have been considerably squeezed together; and the big fold in the centre indicated by dotted lines has been so much compressed in the lower part—that is, in what is now Mont Blanc—that its sides were brought near to each other until they actually sloped inwards instead of outwards.

You may easily imitate this structure by taking a sheet of paper, laying it on the table, and then, putting one hand on each side of it, cause it to rise up in a central fold by pressing your hands towards each other. Notice carefully what happens. First, you get a low arch, or anticline, like that of the Weald. Then as you press it more, the upward fold becomes sharper and narrower; then continue pressing it, and you will find the fold bulging out at the top, but narrowing in below until you get this fan-structure.

This is just what has happened in the case of the Alps. A tremendous lateral pressure applied to the rocks heaved them up and down into great and small folds, and in some places, as in Mont Blanc, fan-structure was produced. Imagine the top of the fan removed, and you get what looks like a syncline, but is really the lower part of a very much compressed anticline.

Now, it is believed that all mountain-ranges have been enormously squeezed by lateral pressure; and the little experiment with the sheet of paper furnishes a good illustration of what has happened. A table-cloth lying on a smooth table will serve equally well. You can easily push it into a series of folds; notice how they come nearer as you continue pushing. You see also that in this way you get long narrow ridges with valleys between. These represent the original anticlines and synclines of mountain-ranges, which in course of time are carved out, as explained above, until the synclines become hills and the anticlines valleys.

Every mountain-chain must originally have had long ridges like these, which in some cases determined the original directions of the streams and valleys; and it is easy to see now why mountain-chains are long and narrow, why their strata have been so greatly folded, and why we get in every mountain-chain long ranges of hills roughly parallel with each other (see chapter vi., pages 177-178).

The reason why granite, gneiss, and crystalline schists are frequently found in the central and highest peaks of mountain-ranges is that we have the oldest and lowest rocks exposed to the surface, on account of the enormous amount of denudation that has taken place. There may be great masses of granite underlying all mountain-chains; but it is only exposed to view when a very great deal of overlying rock has been removed.

It was thought at one time that granite was the oldest of all rocks, and that mountain-chains had been upheaved by masses of granite pushing them up from below; but we know now that both these ideas are mistaken. Some granites are certainly old geologically, but others are of later date; and it is certain that granite was not the upheaving agent, but more likely it followed the overlying rocks as they were heaved up by lateral pressure, because the upward bending of the rocks would tend to relieve the enormous pressure down below, and so the granite would rise up.

MONT BLANC. SNOWFIELDS, GLACIERS. AND STREAMS.

We now pass on to a very different example, where mountains are the result of huge fractures and displacements; namely, the numerous and nearly parallel ranges of the Great Basin, of Western Arizona, and

Northern Mexico. The region between the Sierra Nevada and the Wahsatch Mountains, extending from Idaho to Mexico, is composed of very gently folded rocks deeply buried in places by extensive outflows of lava.

Now, in this case the earth-movements caused great cracks, or splits, doubtless attended by fearful earthquakes. We find here a series of nearly parallel fractures, hundreds of miles long, and fifteen to thirty miles apart. These traverse the entire region, dividing the rocks into long narrow blocks. There is evidence to show that the whole region was once much more elevated than it is now, and has subsided thousands of feet. During the subsidence along these lines of fracture, or faults, the blocks were tilted sideways; and the uptilted blocks, carved by denudation, form the isolated ranges of this very interesting region (see illustration, chap. viii., p. 273, Fig. 1). The faults are indicated by arrows pointing downwards; and the dotted lines indicate the erosion of the uptilted blocks.

But this must be regarded as a very exceptional case, for we do not know of any other mountain-range formed quite in the same way. Why the strata, although only slightly bent, should have snapped so violently in this case, while in other mountain-ranges they have suffered much more bending without so much fracture and displacement, we cannot tell, but can only suggest that possibly it was because they were not buried up under an enormous thickness of overlying rocks, which would exert an enormous downward pressure, and so tend to prevent fracturing.

There are many other deeply interesting questions with regard to the upheaval of mountains which at present cannot be answered.

We have already learned to alter our preconceived ideas about the stability and immovable nature of the earth's crust, and have seen that it is in reality most unstable, and is undergoing continual movements, both great and small. But here we have an equally startling discovery, which quite upsets all our former ideas of the hard and unyielding nature of the rocks composing the earth's crust; for we find that not only can they be bent into innumerable folds and little puckerings, but that in some cases they have been drawn out and squeezed as if they were so much soft putty. The imagination almost fails to grasp such facts as these.

Of late years geologists in Switzerland and in Great Britain have discovered that in some parts of mountains rocks have been enormously distorted and crushed, so that they have assumed very different states from those in which they were made, and curious mineral changes have taken place under the influence of this crushing.

In the very complicated region of the Northwest Highlands of Sutherland and Ross, the structure of which has only lately been explained, some wonderful discoveries of this nature have been made. Certain of the crystalline schists found there have been formed by the crushing down and rearrangement of older rocks that once presented a very different appearance. In this district, where the rocks have been squeezed by enormous lateral pressure, the dislocations sometimes have assumed the form of inclined or undulating planes, the rocks above which have been actually pushed over those below, and in some cases the horizontal displacement amounts to many miles.

Not only have the rocks been ruptured, and older, deep-seated masses been torn up and driven bodily over younger strata (that once were above them), but there has been at the same time such an amount of internal shearing as to crush the rocks into a finely divided material, and to give rise to a streaky arrangement of the broken particles, closely resembling the flow-structure of a lava. In the crushed material new minerals have been sometimes so developed as to produce a true schist.[32]

CHAPTER X.
THE AGES OF MOUNTAINS, AND OTHER QUESTIONS.

O Earth, what changes hast thou seen!

TENNYSON.

It might naturally be asked at what period in the world's primeval or geological history some particular mountain-range was upheaved; whether it is younger or older than another one perhaps not very far away; and again, whether the mountain-chains of the world have been uplifted all at once, or whether the process of elevation was prolonged and gradual?

Questions such as these are deeply interesting, and present to the geologist some of the most fascinating problems to be met with in the whole range of this science. And though at first sight they might seem hopelessly beyond our reach, yet even here the prospect is by no means unpromising; and it is quite possible to show that they can be answered to some extent. Here we shall find our illustration of the cathedral (see chapter v., pages 143-147) holds good once more.

It is perhaps hardly necessary to explain that by looking at a Gothic cathedral one can say at what period or periods it was built. Perhaps it has a Norman nave, with great pillars and rounded arches. Then the chancel might be Early English, with pointed windows and deep mouldings, and other features that serve to mark the style of the building, and therefore its date,—because different styles prevailed at different periods. Other parts might contain work easily recognised as belonging to the "Perpendicular" period.

Now, as there have been periods in the history of architecture and art, so there have been periods in the history of our earth. What these periods were, and how we have learned to recognise them, we must first very briefly describe.[33]

There are two simple rules by which the age of an ordinary sedimentary rock may be ascertained. This is fixed (1) By its position with regard to others; (2) By the nature of its embedded animal or vegetable remains, known as fossils.

These rules may easily be illustrated by a reference to the methods of the antiquary. For instance, suppose you were going to build a house, and the foundations had just been dug out; you might on examining them find several old layers of soil, showing that the site or neighbourhood had been formerly occupied. You might find in one layer stone implements, in another Roman or early British pottery, and yet again portions of brick or stonework, together with tools or articles of domestic use, belonging, say, to the time of Queen Elizabeth. Now, which of these layers would be the oldest? It is quite clear that the lowest layers must have been there the longest, because the others accumulated on the top of them.

The explorations made of late years under Jerusalem have led to the interesting discovery that the modern city is built up on the remains of thirteen former cities of Jerusalem, all of which have been destroyed in one way or another. Here, again, it is quite clear that the oldest layer of débris must be that which lies at the bottom, and the newest will be the one on the top.

Again, you know that the "Stone Age" in Britain came before the Roman occupation. Those old stone implements were made by a barbarous race, who knew very little of agriculture or the arts of civilisation. Then in succeeding centuries various arts were introduced, many relics of which are found buried in the soil; and hence, since different styles of art and architecture prevailed at different periods, the works of art or industry embedded in any old layers of soil serve to fix the date of those layers.

These layers of soil and débris correspond to the layers or strata of the sedimentary rocks, in which the different chapters of the world's history are recorded. Geology is only another kind of history; and the same principles which guide the archæologist searching buried cities also guide the geologist in reading the stony record. As the illustrious Hutton said, "The ruins of an older world are visible in the present state of our planet." The successive layers of ruin in this case are to be seen in the great series of the stratified rocks; and we may lay it down as an axiom that the lowest strata are the oldest, unless by some subsequent disturbance the order should have been reversed, which, fortunately, is a rare occurrence, though examples are to be found in some mountain-chains with violent foldings.

But it often happens that neither the strata which should come above nor those that lie below can be seen. Then our second rule comes in: We can determine the age of the rock in question by its fossils. The reason of this has perhaps already been guessed by the reader. It is that as different kinds of plants and animals have prevailed at different periods of the world's history, so there have been "styles," or fashions, in creation, as well as in art. At one geological period certain curious types of fishes flourished which are now almost extinct, only a few old-fashioned survivals being found in one or two out-of-the-way places. At another period certain types of reptiles flourished vigorously, and were the leaders in their day; but they have altogether vanished and become extinct. So one type after another has appeared on the scene, played its humble part in the great drama of life; and then—"exit!" another takes its place.

In the oldest and lowest of the series of rocks we find no certain trace of life at all. In the next series we find only lowly creatures, such as shell-fish, corals, and crab-like animals that have no backbone. In a higher group of rocks fishes appear for the first time. Later on, we come across the remains of amphibious creatures for the first time. Then follows (after a long unrecorded interval) an era when reptiles and birds existed in great numbers. After another long interval we come to strata containing many and diverse remains of mammals or quadrupeds. So we have an "Age of Fishes," an "Age of Reptiles," and an "Age of Mammals." Some tribes of these creatures died out, but others lived on to the present day. Thus we see that there has been a continuous progress in life as the world grew older, for higher types kept coming in.

To the geologist fossils are of the greatest possible use, since they help him to determine the age of a particular set of strata, for certain kinds of fossils belong to certain rocks, and to them only.

But the classification of the stratified rocks has been carried farther than this. Practical geologists, working in the field, use fossils as their chief guide in working out the subdivisions of a group of rocks, for certain genera and species of old plants and animals are found to belong to certain small groups of strata. In this way a definite order of succession has been established once for all; and, except in the case of inverted strata already alluded to, this order is invariably found to hold good.

This great discovery of the order of succession of the British stratified rocks, established by their fossil contents, is due to William Smith, the father of English geology. After exploring the whole of England, he published in 1815 a geological map, the result of his extraordinary labours. Before then people had no idea of a definite and regular succession of rocks extending over the country, capable of being recognised to some extent by the nature of the rocks themselves,—whether sandstones, clays, or limestones, etc., but chiefly by their own fossils. They thought the different kinds of rocks were scattered promiscuously up and down the face of the country; but now we know that they do not show themselves in this haphazard way, but have definite relations to each other, like the many volumes of one large book.

By combining the two principles referred to above, geologists have arranged the great series of British stratified rocks into certain groups, each indicating a long period of time. First, they are roughly divided into three large groups, marking the three great eras into which geological time is divided. Secondly, these eras are further divided into certain periods. These periods are again divided into epochs, indicated by local divisions of their rocks. In this way we have something like a historical table. Omitting the small epochs of time, this table is as follows, in descending order:—

Table of the British Stratified Rocks.

ERA.　　　PERIOD. PREVAILING TYPE.

Era	Period	Prevailing Type
Cainozoic or Tertiary	Recent. Pleistocene, or Quaternary. Pliocene. Miocene. Eocene.	Mammals.
Mesozoic, or Secondary.	Cretaceous. Neocomian. Jurassic. Triassic. Permian.	Reptiles
Palæozoic, or Primary.	Carboniferous. Devonian, and Old Red Sandstone. Silurian. Cambrian. Archæan,[34] or Pew-Cambrian.	Fishes. Creatures without a backbone (invertebrates).

The total thickness of all these rocks has been estimated at about one hundred thousand feet, or not far from twenty miles. These names have been given partly from the region in which the rocks occur, partly from the nature of the rocks themselves, and partly for other reasons. Thus the Old Red Sandstone is so called, because it generally, though not always, appears as a dark red sandstone. But the Silurian rocks, which we find in North Wales, receive their name from the Silures, an ancient Welsh tribe; the Cambrian rocks take theirs from Cambria, the old name for North Wales. The Cretaceous rocks are partly composed of chalk, for which the Latin word is creta; and so on. The terms "Palæozoic," "Mesozoic," and "Cainozoic" mean "ancient life," "middle life," and "recent or new life," thus indicating that as time went on the various types of life that flourished on the earth became less old-fashioned, and more like those prevailing at the present time. These used to be called "Primary," "Secondary," and "Tertiary;" but the terms were unfortunate, because the primary rocks, as then known, were not the first, or oldest. We have therefore included the Archæan rocks, since discovered, in this primary group. Only one fossil has been found in these rocks, and that is a doubtful one; hence they are sometimes called "Azoic," that is, "without life." The Mesozoic rocks are, as it were, the records of the "middle ages" in the world's history; while the Palæozoic take us back to a truly primeval time.

We have now learned how the geological age of any group of rocks may be determined. Thus, if a series of rocks of unknown age can be shown to rest on undoubtedly Silurian rocks in one place, and in another place to be overlaid or covered by undoubtedly Carboniferous rocks, they will probably belong to the Old Red Sandstone Period. If afterwards we find that they contain some of the well-known fossils of that period, the question of their age is settled at once. But we want more evidence than this. Suppose, now, we find somewhere on the flanks of a mountain-range a series of Permian and Triassic rocks, resting almost horizontally on disturbed and folded Carboniferous strata. Does not that at once prove that the upheaval took place before the Permian Period? Clearly it does, because the Permian rocks have evidently not been disturbed thereby. So now we can fix the date of our range of hills; namely, after the Carboniferous Period and before the Permian Period.

It is by such reasoning that the age of our Pennine range of hills, extending from the north of England into Derbyshire, has been fixed; for the Permian and Triassic strata lie undisturbed on the upheaved arch of Carboniferous rocks of which this chain is composed. Its structure is that of a broken and much denuded anticline, which stands up to form a line of hills only because the Carboniferous limestone is so much harder than the "coal measures," or coal-bearing rocks, on each side of it, that it has not been worn away so fast. In time, this great anticline will be entirely worn away like that of the Weald. It is called the Great Mountain Limestone, because it so often rises up to form high ground. The Mendip Hills in Somersetshire are of about the same date, and they too are largely composed of this great limestone formation.

Of course, a certain amount of up and down movement took place after the hills were upheaved, otherwise the Permian and Triassic rocks could not have been deposited on their sides; but these movements were slight and of a more general kind than those by which strata are thrown into folds.

The main upheaval, by which the rocks now forming the Highlands of Scotland were lifted up and contorted, took place after the Lower Silurian Period, and before that of the Old Red Sandstone; and there is clear evidence that even before the latter period they had not only been greatly altered, or "metamorphosed," by subterranean heat, but that they had suffered enormous denudation. And the work of carving out these mountains has gone on ever since; for even in Old Red Sandstone times they were probably not entirely covered by water. The Highland Mountains are therefore older than the Pennine range.

Geologically Scotland belongs in great part to Scandinavia; and the long line of Scandinavian Mountains is a continuation of the Highlands, and so is of the same age.

Mountain-chains and hill-ranges have been upheaved at various geological periods; and some are very old, while others are much younger.

Turning to the southeast of England, we find the ranges of chalk hills forming the North and South Downs (see page 237). As explained previously, these owe their existence to the upheaval and subsequent denudation of the low arch, or anticline, of the Weald. They are called "escarpments," because they are like lines of cliffs that are being gradually cut back. Now, it is clear that these hills are much newer than either of those we have just considered. Look at the table on page 324, and you will see that the Cretaceous rocks (chalk, etc.) belong to the Mesozoic era. The chalk was the last rock formed during the Cretaceous Period.

So the Wealden arch must have been heaved up after the chalk was formed; that is, ages and ages later than the date of the Pennine range or the Scotch Highlands. From other evidences it has been shown that this anticline was heaved up in the early part of the Cainozoic Era, perhaps during the Miocene Period.

Let us now take the case of the Alps. And here we have an instructive example of a great mountain system formed by repeated movements during a long succession of geological periods. We cannot say that they were entirely raised up at any one time in the world's past history. In the centre of this great range we find a series of igneous and metamorphic rocks, such as granite, gneiss, and crystalline schists. Some of these may belong to the very oldest period,—namely, the Archæan; others are probably Palæozoic and Cainozoic deposits greatly altered by heat and pressure.

The ground from Savoy to Austria began to be an area of disturbance and upheaval towards the close of the Palæozoic Era, if not before; so that crystalline schists and Carboniferous strata were raised up to form elevated land around which Permian conglomerates and shingle-beds were formed,—as on the seashore at the present day.

During the early part of the Mesozoic Era local fractures and certain up and down movements occurred. After this there was a long period of subsidence, during which a series of strata known as Oölites and Cretaceous were deposited on the floor of an old sea.

Towards the close of this long era, a fresh upheaval took place along the present line of the Alps,—an upheaval that was prolonged into the Eocene Period. It was during this latter period that a very extensive formation known as the "Nummulitic limestone" was formed in a sea that covered a large part of Europe and Asia. We have already referred (see chap. v., pp. 169-171) to the way in which limestones have been formed. Nummulites are little shells that were formed by tiny shell-fish.

But after this, the greatest upheaval and disturbance took place,—an upheaval to which the Alps as we now see them are chiefly due. By this means the older Cainozoic strata, once lying horizontally on the floor of the sea, were raised up, together with older rocks, to form dry land, and not only raised up, but crumpled, dislocated, and in some cases turned upside down.

So intense was the compression to which the Eocene rocks were subjected that they were converted into a hard and even crystalline state. It seems almost incredible that these highly altered rocks which look so ancient are of the same date as our London clay and the soft Eocene deposits of the south of England; but in our country the movement that raised up those strata was of the most feeble and gentle kind compared to the violent disturbances that took place in Switzerland.

And here we may point out that the Alps are only a portion of a vast chain of mountains stretching right across Europe and Asia in a general east and west direction, beginning with the Pyrenees and passing through the Alps, the Carpathians, the Caucasus, and the range of Elbruz to the Hindoo-Koosh and the high plateau of Pamir, called "the roof of the world," which stands like a huge fortress, fifteen thousand feet high. Thence it passes to the still higher tracts of Thibet, great plains exceeding in height the highest summits of the Alps, being enclosed between the lofty ramparts of the Himalayas on the south and the Kuen-Lun Mountains on the north; and thence the mountain wall is prolonged in the Yuen-Ling, In-Shan, Khin-Gan, and other ranges till it finally passes to the Pacific Ocean at Behring's Strait.

All these ranges are, as it were, the backbone of the great continental plateau of the Old World, and doubtless are chiefly due to those earth-movements by means of which the Alps were upheaved. The last grand movement, which raised the Mont Blanc range, was probably rather later, and seems to have taken place as late as the Pliocene Period.

At the present day no great movements are taking place in the Alps; but now and then earthquakes visit this region, and serve to remind us that the process of mountain-making is still slowly going on.

Probably there have been times in the history of all these mountain-ranges when movements took place of a more violent and convulsive kind than anything with which we are familiar at the present day; and the age we live in may be one of comparative repose. This is of course somewhat a matter of speculation; and we only allude to it because there has been a tendency on the part of some to carry the theory of uniformity in all geological operations much farther than Hutton or Lyell ever intended. But at the same time there is no need to go back to the old teaching of sudden catastrophes and violent revolutions. We only wish to avoid either of these two extremes and to take a safe middle course.

How rapidly some of these great earth-movements took place it is impossible at present to say; but in several cases it can be shown that they were quite slow, as indicated by the testimony of the rivers. Thus, the rise of the great Uintah Mountains of the Western States was so slow and gradual that the Green River, which flowed across the site of the range, so far from being turned aside as they rose up, has actually been able to deepen its cañon as fast as the mountains were upheaved. So that the two processes, as it were, kept pace with each other, and the river went on cutting out its gorges at the same time that the ground over which it flowed was gently upheaved; and as the land rose the river flowed faster, and therefore acquired more power to cut and deepen its channel. This is a valuable piece of evidence; but in this case we have only a few big broad folds, instead of the violent folding seen in the Alps. However, certain Pliocene strata lying on the southern flanks of the Himalayas show that the rivers still run in the same lines as they occupied before the last great upheaval took place.

We have seen how the substance of the mountains was slowly manufactured by means of such quiet and gentle operations as may be witnessed at the present day; how the rivers of old brought down their burdens as they do now, and flung them into the sea; how the sea spread them out very slowly and compacted them into level layers, to form, in process of time, the hard rocky framework of the plateaux, hills, and mountains of the world; how vast marine accumulations were also slowly manufactured through the agency of countless generations of humble organisms, subtracting carbonate of lime from sea water to form the limestones of future ages; how by slow earth-movements these marine deposits were reared up into dry land; how they have frequently been penetrated by molten rocky matter from below, which occasionally forced its way up to the surface and gave rise to various volcanic eruptions, by means of which the sedimentary rocks were often considerably baked and hardened, and new fissures filled up with valuable metallic ores and precious stones; how lava-flows and great deposits of volcanic ash were mingled with these sedimentary rocks.

Then we endeavoured to follow the history of these rocky layers after their upheaval, and learn how they are affected by the ceaseless operations of rain and rivers and other agents of destruction, so that finally the upheaved ridges of the lands are carved out into all those wonderful features of crag and pinnacle and precipice that give the mountains their present shapes and outlines. All this we were able to account for, without the aid of any imaginary or unnatural causes.

And, lastly, we have seen that even where such causes might seem at first almost indispensable,—when mountains tell us of mighty internal forces crumpling, folding, and fracturing their rocky framework,—yet even there we can account for what we see without supposing them to have been torn and tossed about by any very violent convulsions.

MOUNTAIN IN THE YOSEMITE VALLEY.

Although the question of the cause, or causes, of earth-movements, whereby continents are upheaved, and the contorting, folding, and crumpling of the rocks of mountains produced, is not at present thoroughly explained, it may perhaps be worth our while to consider briefly some of the views that have been put forward on this difficult subject. The words "upheaval" and "elevation," in reference to movements of the earth's surface, are somewhat misleading, but are used for want of better terms. They would seem to imply that the force which produced mountains was a kind of upward push; whereas, in most cases, and perhaps in all, the force, whatever it was, did not act in an upward direction. So it should be understood that we employ these terms only to indicate that the rocks have somehow been carried up to a higher level, and not as suggesting how the force acted by which they were raised.

It seems pretty clear that in the case of mountain-chains, at least, the force acted in a horizontal direction, as a kind of side-thrust.

This we endeavoured to illustrate in chapter ix. by means of a simple experiment with a sheet of paper; and it was shown how folds similar to those of which Mont Blanc is composed could be imitated by simply pressing the sides of a sheet of paper inwards with one's two hands as it lies on a table. Such lateral pressure, it is thought by many, must be caused by the shrinking of the lower and hotter parts of the earth's crust as they cool, leaving the outer crust unsupported, so that it gradually settles down onto a smaller surface below, and in so doing must inevitably be wrinkled and throw itself into a series of folds (see chapter vi., page 204).

The interior of the earth is hotter than the outside; and since there is good reason to think that the whole earth was once upon a time in a highly heated and perhaps half molten condition, we are compelled to believe that it always has been, and still is, a cooling globe. Now, almost all known substances are found to contract more or less on cooling; and so if the materials of which the earth is mainly composed are at all similar in their nature and properties to those which we find on its surface, it follows that the earth must be contracting at the same time that it is cooling, just as a red-hot poker will contract on being taken out of the fire.

Moreover, we find that hot bodies contract faster than those that are merely warm, so that a red-hot poker contracts more during the first few minutes after it is taken out of the fire than it does after it has passed the red-hot stage. Hence it is easy to see that the interior portions of the earth, which are hotter, must be contracting at a greater rate than its external parts, for they evidently have very little heat to lose. This may seem rather puzzling to the reader at first; for it might be argued that the heat from below must pass through the external layers, or crust, as it is often called. But it should be remembered that this is not the only way in which the earth loses heat. Think of the vast amount of heat given out from the earth every year by volcanic eruptions, and you will see at once that much of the cooling takes place in this way, and not as a direct flow of heat from the interior, as in the case of the poker. A single big lava-stream flowing out from a volcano, and cooling on the surface of the earth, represents so much heat lost forever; and so do the clouds of steam emitted during every eruption; so, again, do even the hot springs that are continually bringing up warm water. If, then, the lower portions of the earth are slowly contracting, they must tend to leave the outer portions of the crust unsupported, so that they would be compelled by their own enormous weight to settle down. Now, we know that something like this happens in coal mines; and as long passages are hollowed out below, the ground begins to "creep," or slowly sink. Think what would be the effect of a slow sinking of any portion of the earth down towards the centre; it would inevitably be curved up and down into numerous folds, as it endeavoured to get itself onto a smaller space, much in the same way that a table-cloth, when thrown onto a table in a kind of arch, settles down in a series of waves, or folds. And this, it is thought, is the way in which it happens that the pressure comes, as we said just now, sideways, instead of from below upwards. It is on this theory that many geologists account for the enormous side-pressure to which rocks have in many cases been subjected.

The evidences of such pressure are many. In some cases fossils have been thereby pulled out of shape and appear considerably distorted; in others, even hard quartz pebbles have been considerably elongated (see chap. ix., pp. 315-316). Then again, we have the little crumplings of all sizes so frequently seen in mica-schists. And lastly, the peculiar property that slates possess of splitting up into thin sheets is found to be due to the same cause; namely, lateral pressure. Slates were originally formed of soft dark mud, and on being subsequently squeezed, by earth-movements, have assumed a structure known as "cleavage," whereby their tiny mud-particles were elongated, and all assumed the same direction, thus giving to the rock this peculiar property of splitting. It can be proved that the pressure came in a direction opposite to that of the planes of cleavage; and it is found that the direction of the cleavage corresponds in a general way with the direction, or trend, of a mountain-chain which is composed partly of slates, as in North Wales. And this discovery helps and harmonises with what we have already said about the cause of the folds in mountain-chains, for the same force, acting sideways, produced the cleavage and the folding, etc.

It has been already stated that in a large number of cases a mountain-range has a central axis, or band, of granite or other crystalline rock. This led some people to suppose that the granite had been driven up from below, and in so doing had thrust up the overlying rocks seen on either flank of the chain; in other words, they believed granite to have been the upheaving agent. And even now we often find unscientific writers speaking of the volcanic forces of upheaval.

Having very little idea of the true structure of mountains, they believed them to consist of a kind of core, or axis, of this igneous rock, with sedimentary rocks sloping away from it on each side. This was a very simple theory of mountain-chains, but unfortunately it will not bear examination. It takes no notice of the folding which is so characteristic of mountain strata, and is quite out of agreement with the facts of the case; so it must be buried among the archives of the past. Mountain-chains are now known to have a much more complicated structure than this,—thanks to the labours of many subsequent observers.

That illustrious astronomer, the late Sir John Herschel, threw out a bold suggestion on this subject, which in the light of recent discoveries with regard to the delicate adjustment between the internal and external forces affecting the earth's surface, is worthy of careful consideration. His idea was that the mere weight of a thick mass of sediment resting on any portion of the earth's crust might cause a certain amount of sinking; and that this would cause portions on either side to swell up. It is certain that as great deposits of sedimentary materials accumulate on the floor of an ocean, that floor slowly sinks, otherwise the sea would become choked up, and dry land would take its place. Now, it is found that every great mountain-chain consists of many thousands of feet of strata thus formed; and more than this: it turns out that a greater thickness of such materials has been formed in regions where we now see mountain-chains than in those continental regions that lie farther away from them. This is an important fact, which was not known in Sir John Herschel's time. One striking example may be mentioned here. In the complicated region of the Appalachian chain the strata are estimated to have a total thickness of eight miles; while in Indiana, where the same strata are nearly horizontal, they are less than one mile thick. Hence it is not impossible that in the mere accumulation, through long periods of time, of vast masses of strata many thousands of feet thick, we may find a potent cause of earth-movements.

The marginal regions of oceans, where most deposition takes place, seem to undergo slow subsidence, while the continents seem in most places to be as slowly rising. Modern geologists are inclined to think that as denudation wears down a continental surface, removing from it a great quantity of solid rocky matter (see chap. v., pp. 161-163), the pressure below is somewhat lessened, or in other words, so much weight is taken off; but that, on the other hand, as this extra amount of material accumulates on the bed of a neighbouring ocean the pressure is increased by a corresponding amount, and so the balance between internal and external forces is upset, and movements consequently take place. We have already seen that the external parts of the earth are much more subject to movements than might have been expected; and for our part, we are willing to believe that in this simple way upheaving forces might be called into play sufficient to account for even the elevation of mountain-chains. For suppose a great mass of strata to continue sinking as they were formed, for long periods of time; what seems to follow? The downward movement would go on until a time would come when the strata, in endeavouring to settle down at a lower level, would (as by the contraction theory above explained) be forced to fold themselves into ridges, and in this way long strips of them might even be elevated into mountain-ranges.

Another ingenious idea was suggested by the late Mr. Scrope, whose work on volcanoes is well known. His idea was that when a large amount of sedimentary material has accumulated on any large area of the bed of the ocean, it somewhat checks the flow of heat from within, and therefore the temperature of the rocks forming part of the earth's crust below will be increased, much in the same manner as a glove checks the escape of heat from the hand and keeps it warm. The consequence of this would be expansion; and as such expansion would be chiefly in a horizontal direction, the area would bulge upwards and cause elevation of the strata resting on it. But there are several difficulties which this theory fails to explain.

And lastly, Professor Le Conte, holding that the contraction theory is unsatisfactory, accounts for earth-movements of all kinds by supposing that some internal parts of the earth cool and contract faster than others. Those parts that cool fastest, according to this theory, are those that underlie the oceanic basins or troughs; while the continental areas, not cooling so rapidly, are left standing up in relief. This theory, which does not seem very satisfactory, is based upon the idea that some parts of the earth's interior may be capable of conducting heat faster than others. We know that some substances, like iron, are good conductors of heat, while others are bad conductors; and it is therefore conceivable that heat may be flowing faster along some parts of the earth than along others; and if so, there would be differences in the rate of contraction.

There are various theories with regard to the nature of the earth's interior. One of these already referred to, but now antiquated, supposes our planet to consist of a thin, solid crust lying on a molten interior, so that the world would be something like an egg with its thin shell and liquid, or semi-liquid, interior. Now, there are grave reasons for refusing to accept this idea. In the first place, a certain slow movement of the earth known as "precession," because it causes the precession of the equinoctial points on the earth's orbit, could not possibly take place as it does if the earth's interior were in this loose and molten condition. That is a matter decided by mathematical calculation, on which we will not dwell further. Secondly, we obtain some very valuable evidence on this abstruse subject from the well-known daily phenomenon of the tides, caused, as the reader is probably aware, by the attractions of the sun and moon; but much more by the moon, because she is nearer, and so exerts a greater pull on the ocean as each part of the world is brought directly under her by the earth's daily rotation on its axis. The waters of our oceans rise up twice each day as they get in a line with the moon, and then begin to fall again. Thus we get that daily ebb and flow seen on our shores. Now, it has been clearly proved by Sir William Thomson, and others, that if any considerable portion of the interior of the earth were in a fluid condition, it too would rise and fall every day as the ocean does. So we should in that case have a tide below the earth as well as on its surface, and the one would tend to neutralise the other, and the ocean tide ought to appear less than it actually is. Even if the earth's crust were made of solid steel, and several hundreds of miles thick, it would yield so much to the enormous pulls exerted by both the sun and moon that it would simply carry the waters of the ocean up and down with it, and we should therefore see no appreciable rise and fall of the water relatively to the land. As a matter of fact, there is a very slight tide in the solid earth below our feet, but so slight that it does not practically affect the tide which we see every day in the ocean. But we wish to show that were the interior of the earth in anything approaching, to a fluid or molten condition, the phenomena of the tides would be very different from what they actually are.

All geologists are therefore agreed that we must consider our earth as a more or less solid body, and not as being something like an india-rubber ball filled with water.

The only question is whether it is entirely solid throughout. Some authorities consider this to be the case. But others venture to think that while the great mass of the globe is solid, there may be a thin liquid layer lying somewhere below the surface. Sir William Thomson calculates that there must be a solid crust at least two thousand or twenty-five hundred miles thick (the diameter of the earth is about eight thousand miles) and that the mass of the earth "is on the whole more rigid certainly than a continuous solid globe of glass of the same diameter."

One other question with regard to the earth's interior may be mentioned in conclusion. Astronomers have calculated the weight of our planet, and the result is curious; for it turns out to be at least twice as heavy as the heaviest rocks that are found on or near the surface. It is about five and a half times as heavy as a globe of water of the same size would be, whereas most rocks with which we are acquainted are about two and a half, or at most three times heavier than water. This fact seems to open out curious consequences; for instance, it is quite possible that metals (which are of course much heavier than water) may exist in the earth's interior in considerable quantities. The imagination at once conjures up vast quantities of gold and silver. What is the source of the gold and silver, and other metals found in mineral veins? This question cannot as yet be fully answered. Very small quantities of various metals have been detected in sea-water; and so some geologists look upon the sea as the source from which metals came. But it is possible that they were introduced from below,—perhaps by the action of steam and highly heated water during periods of volcanic activity,—and that their source is far down below in the depths of the earth.

But perhaps we have already wandered too far into the regions of speculation.

Such are some of the interesting problems suggested by the study of mountains, and they add no small charm to the science of geology.

And as we leave the mountains behind us, refreshed by their bracing air, and strengthened for another season of toil and labour by a brief sojourn among their peaks and passes, we come away with a renewed sense of the almost unlimited power of the unhasting operations of Nature, and the wisdom and beneficence of the Great Architect of the Universe, who made and planned those snowcapped temples as symbols of His strength, who was working millions of years ago as He is working to-day, and to whom a thousand years are as one day.

FOOTNOTES:

[1] Published by Messrs. Spooner, of the Strand.

[2] Epic of Hades.

[3] Modern Painters, vol. iv.

[4] Scenery of Scotland.

[5] Modern Painters, vol. iv.

[6] "The Alpine Regions of Switzerland" (Deighton, Bell, & Co.), a most interesting book, especially for travellers.

[7] It has lately been proved that clouds can only form in air which contains dust, and that each little suspended particle of water contains a speck of dust or a tiny germ of some sort for its nucleus.

[8] Pressure also has an important influence, but was omitted above for the sake of simplicity.

[9] Ruskin, "Modern Painters."

[10] The Alpine Regions of Switzerland.

[11] Mountaineering in 1861 (Longman).

[12] Mr. R. S. Watson, in "The Alpine Journal," vol. i., p. 143.

[13] Conservateur Suisse, xlvi. p. 478, vol. xii.

[14] Bonney.

[15] The word "Alpine" is used in a general sense to denote the vegetation that grows naturally on the most elevated regions of the earth; that is, on all high mountains, whether they rise up in hot tropical plains or in cooler northern pastures.

[16] The following remarks are largely taken from the Introduction to Ball's well-known "Alpine Guide."

[17] Flowerless in the ordinary, not the botanical sense.

[18] We are again indebted to Professor Bonney's "Alpine Regions of Switzerland" for the information here given.

[19] Bonar on Chamois-hunting in Bavaria.

[20] The reader will find an account of the old red sandstone in the writer's "Autobiography of the Earth" (Edward Stanford, 1890).

[21] The flints usually found in limestone are also of organic origin.

[22] Schists are so named from their property of splitting into thin layers. Their structure is crystalline; and the layers, or folia, consist usually of two or more minerals, but sometimes of only one. Thus mica-schist consists of quartz and mica, each arranged in many folia, but it splits along the layers of mica.

[23] Modern Painters.

[24] Modern Painters.

[25] See papers by the writer on Volcanoes and Volcanic Action in "Knowledge" for May and June, 1891, on which this chapter is partly based.

[26] Perhaps these Scripture phrases were suggested long before the Bible was written, by the sight of some crater in active eruption.

[27] The Hawaiian Archipelago.

[28] "The Crest of the Continent," by Ernest Ingersoll, Chicago, 1885.

[29] Scenery of Scotland page 130, new edition.

[30] Bonney.

[31] Scenery of Scotland, page 201, new edition.

[32] Geikie.

[33] For a fuller account see the writer's "Autobiography of the Earth."

[34] The Archæan rocks are frequently placed in a separate group below the Palæozoic.

Milton Keynes UK
Ingram Content Group UK Ltd.
UKHW030907151124
451262UK00006B/945

and the large quantity of bones and coins that have been found proves that the fall was so sudden that the inhabitants had no time to escape.

Taurentum, another Roman town, situated, it is said, on the banks of Lake Geneva, at the base of one of the spurs of the Dent d'Oche, was completely crushed in A. D. 563 by a downfall of rocks. The sloping heap of débris thus formed may still be seen advancing like a headland into the waters of the lake. A terrible flood-wave, produced by the deluge of stones, reached the opposite shores of the lake and swept away all the inhabitants. Every town and village on the banks, from Morges to Vevay, was demolished, and they did not begin the work of rebuilding till the following century. Some say, however, that the disaster was caused by a landslip which fell from the Grammont or Derochiaz across the valley of the Rhone, just above the spot where it flows into the Lake of Geneva. Hundreds of such falls have taken place within the Alps and neighbouring mountains within historic times.

Two out of the five peaks of the Diablerets fell down, one in 1714 and the other in 1749, covering the pastures with a thick layer of stones and earth more than three hundred feet thick, and by obstructing the course of the stream of Lizerne, formed the three lakes of Derborence. In like manner the Bernina, the Dent du Midi, the Dent de Mayen, and the Righi have overspread with ruin vast tracts of cultivated land. In Switzerland the most noted Bergfalls are those from the Diablerets and the Rossberg. The former mountain is a long flattish ridge with several small peaks, overhanging very steep walls of rock on either side. These walls are composed of alternating beds of limestone and shale. Hence it is easily perceived that we have here conditions favourable for landslips, because if anything weakens one of these beds of shale the overlying mass might be inclined to break away. The fall in the year 1714, already referred to, was a very destructive one.

THE MATTERHORN. FROM A PHOTOGRAPH BY MR. DONKIN.

"For two whole days previously loud groaning had been heard to issue from the mountain, as though some imprisoned spirit were struggling to release himself, like Typhœus from under Etna; then a vast fragment of the upper part of the mountain broke suddenly away and thundered down the precipices into the valley beneath. In a few minutes fifty-five châlets, with sixteen men and many head of cattle, were buried for ever under the ruins. One remarkable escape has indeed been recorded, perhaps the most marvellous ever known. A solitary herdsman from the village of Avent occupied one of the châlets which were buried under the fallen mass. Not a trace of it remained; his friends in the valley below returned from their unsuccessful search, and mourned him as dead. He was, however, still among the living; a huge rock had fallen in such a manner as to protect the roof of his châlet, which, as is often the case, rested against a cliff. Above this, stones and earth had accumulated, and the man was buried alive. Death would soon have released him from his imprisonment, had not a little rill of water forced its way through the débris and trickled into the châlet. Supported by this and by his store of cheese, he lived three months, labouring all the while incessantly to escape. Shortly before Christmas he succeeded, after almost incredible toil, in once more looking on the light of day, which his dazzled eyes, so long accustomed to the murky darkness below, for a while could scarcely support. He hastened down to his home in Avent, and knocked at his own door; pale and haggard, he scarcely seemed a being of this world. His relations would not believe that one so long lost could yet be alive, and the door was shut in his face. He turned to